# WOOD FINISHING 101
## The STEP-BY-STEP GUIDE

## BOB FLEXNER
Author of *Understanding Wood Finishing*

**POPULAR WOODWORKING BOOKS**
CINCINNATI, OHIO
www.popularwoodworking.com

## READ THIS IMPORTANT SAFETY NOTICE

To prevent accidents, keep safety in mind while you work. Use the safety guards installed on power equipment; they are for your protection.

When working on power equipment, keep fingers away from saw blades, wear safety goggles to prevent injuries from flying wood chips and sawdust, wear hearing protection and consider installing a dust vacuum to reduce the amount of airborne sawdust in your woodshop.

Don't wear loose clothing, such as neckties or shirts with loose sleeves, or jewelry, such as rings, necklaces or bracelets, when working on power equipment. Tie back long hair to prevent it from getting caught in your equipment.

People who are sensitive to certain chemicals should check the chemical content of any product before using it.

Due to the variability of local conditions, construction materials, skill levels, etc., neither the author nor Popular Woodworking Books assumes any responsibility for any accidents, injuries, damages or other losses incurred resulting from the material presented in this book.

The authors and editors who compiled this book have tried to make the contents as accurate and correct as possible. Plans, illustrations, photographs and text have been carefully checked. All instructions, plans and projects should be carefully read, studied and understood before beginning construction.

Prices listed for supplies and equipment were current at the time of publication and are subject to change.

## METRIC CONVERSION CHART

| TO CONVERT | TO | MULTIPLY BY |
|---|---|---|
| Inches | Centimeters | 2.54 |
| Centimeters | Inches | 0.4 |
| Feet | Centimeters | 30.5 |
| Centimeters | Feet | 0.03 |
| Yards | Meters | 0.9 |
| Meters | Yards | 1.1 |

Distributed in Canada by Fraser Direct
100 Armstrong Avenue
Georgetown, Ontario L7G 5S4
Canada

Distributed in the U.K. and Europe by F+W Media International
Brunel House
Newton Abbot
Devon TQ12 4PU
England
Tel: (+44) 1626 323200
Fax: (+44) 1626 323319
E-mail: postmaster@davidandcharles.co.uk

Distributed in Australia by Capricorn Link
P.O. Box 704
Windsor, NSW 2756
Australia

Visit our Web site at www.popularwoodworking.com.

Other fine Popular Woodworking Books are available from your local bookstore or direct from the publisher.

Acquisitions editor: David Thiel
Designer: Brian Roeth
Production coordinator: Mark Griffin

**ABOUT THE AUTHOR**

Bob Flexner has operated his own furniture making and restoration shop in Norman, OK for 35 years. For the last 20 years, he has taught wood finishing and restoration. His writing accomplishments include the authoritative and best-selling book, *Understanding Wood Finishing*, now in its second edition, editing the professional trade magazine *Finishing and Restoration*, making the award-winning DVDs, "Repairing Furniture" and "Refinishing Furniture" for Taunton Press, and writing the long-running columns "Finishing" in *Woodshop News*, and "Flexner on Finishing" in *Popular Woodworking Magazine*, now in book form by the same name.

# Welcome to Wood Finishing 101

Every now and then a beginning woodworker or home hobbyist asks me to recommend a book on finishing, and I always feel a little hesitant because finishing books are written for the broad audience — beginner through advanced. (It's a marketing thing.) They're never written just for the beginner, who wants simple finishes and step-by-step procedures. The result is, the beginner gets bogged down in information overload.

This is the missing book — the book for beginners. A step-by-step picture book focused on how to apply the most common stains and finishes.

I have included, however, brief (three pages each) overviews of stains and finishes right at the beginning to help you put all the products and procedures in perspective. There are also overviews of solvents, wood, and several other topics I hope you find informative and interesting later in the book. Otherwise, this book is "step-by-step."

If you choose, you can skip these stain-and-finish overviews and go straight to the section you are interested in. Each chapter is self-contained.

Applying finishes is easy and logical. I do have one caution, however. Don't be impatient. Stains and finishes take awhile to dry, overnight in many cases. It doesn't take much time to apply the product, but you need to allow time for drying in a warm area before proceeding to the next step. Impatience is probably the beginner's most challenging obstacle.

The book is designed as a series of exercises, to be done on practice panels. The goal here is to give you the experience and confidence to proceed to an actual project. But applying finishes isn't difficult, so there's no reason not to proceed directly to the project itself.

If you do choose some exercises, you can do them on scrap wood, or you can buy a full sheet of veneered plywood or MDF (medium-density fiberboard), and cut it into smaller sections.

In the construction trade, it's common to hear the carpenters rationalize their sloppiness with the defense, "Oh, the painters will fix it." In the same sense, it's the finishing of a project that makes it beautiful and a success. A poor finish is a failed project. A great finish is admired. I hope this book helps you achieve admired status.

I want to thank my son, Soren, for giving me the idea for this book and my brother, Bill, for getting me back on track. I also want to thank my wife, Birthe, for her steady support and my editor, David Thiel, for his patience with me.

*Bob Flexner*

# TABLE OF CONTENTS

# Understanding Stains

## Stains and Staining

### DEFINITION

A stain is a colorant (pigment or dye) and a binder (some sort of finish) with a lot of thinner added so the excess stain is easy to wipe off. This leaves some color in or on the wood.

A stain can also be just dye and thinner with no binder added.

### PIGMENT

Pigment is ground earth or colored synthetic particles, so pigment requires a binder to glue it to the wood. Pigment settles to the bottom of the can and has to be stirred into suspension before use.

### DYE

Dye is a colorant dissolved in a liquid, so dye penetrates well and doesn't need a binder. Coffee and tea are examples of weak dyes.

### PURPOSE OF A STAIN

There are three good reasons to use a stain:

1. To make a cheaper, less interesting (usually lighter) wood look like a more expensive (usually darker) wood such as walnut, cherry or mahogany.
2. To match the color of an existing object.
3. To create a décor you or someone else has in mind.

### TYPES OF STAIN

Common categories of wood stain include:

- Oil stain (thins and cleans up with mineral spirits).
- Water-based stain (thins and cleans up with water).

Pigment settles to the bottom of the can and has to be stirred.

One of the principal reasons to stain wood, especially lighter woods, is to make them resemble more desirable darker woods, in this case walnut (on the right).

There are five common types of stain. From left to right are examples of oil stain, water-based stain, gel stain, two types of dye stain (concentrated and thinned liquid, and powder), and combination stain and varnish.

- Gel stain (thick in the can like mayonnaise but spreads and wipes off easily).
- Dye stain (a colorant dissolved in a liquid).
- Combination stain and finish (doesn't color effectively if wiped off and is streaky with brush marks if brushed and left thick).

The primary differences in stains are as follows:

- *Ease of application.* Oil stains are the easiest to apply because you have plenty of time to wipe off the excess. All the other stains dry quickly so you have to work fast or on smaller areas at a time.
- *Drying time.* Dye stains dissolved in solvent (not water), can be coated over within minutes. Water-based stains can be coated over after about an hour. Gel stains, and dyes dissolved in water, require 4 to 6 hours before coating over. Oil stains should be allowed overnight drying.
- *Grain definition.* All stains provide good grain definition if the excess is wiped off, because more colorant is left in the grain. Dye stains produce slightly less definition than pigment stains.
- *Color control.* Dye stains provide the best control of color — that is, getting the color darker without obscuring the figure of the wood. Dye is see-through; you can apply as

The basic rule for applying all stains is to apply a wet coat and wipe off the excess before it dries. It's much faster to apply stain with a cloth than a brush.

many coats as you want and still see the wood's figure. Pigment hides the wood's figure if built up.

## STAIN APPLICATION

The basic rule for applying all stains is to apply a wet coat and wipe off the excess before the stain dries. Unless the wood is naturally blotch-prone or you haven't sanded the wood well enough to remove all gouges and scratches, you will always get an even coloring.

You may need to divide your project into smaller sections, or have a second person wipe as you apply, to get good results using one of the faster drying stains. It's much faster to wipe the stain onto the wood with a cloth, wearing gloves of course, than to brush it. (I can't remember ever brushing a stain.)

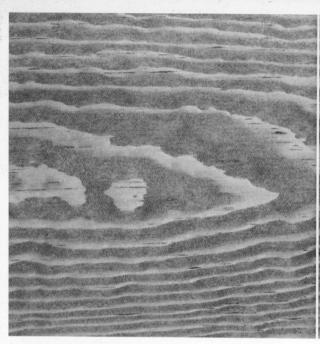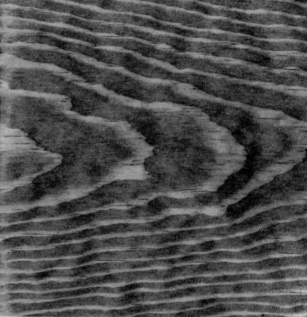

A washcoat, which is any finish thinned to about 10% solids, can be used to reduce blotching, but it also reduces the intensity of the stain's color. On this sample, I applied a varnish washcoat (wood con- ditioner) to the left side of the pine panel and let it dry overnight. Then I applied a stain to the entire panel.

## APPLICATION PROBLEMS

Common problems and ways to avoid them:

- The stain dries in spots before you get it all wiped off, leaving an uneven coloring. If you are quick enough, you can wipe more stain on smaller sections at a time to reliquify the stain so you can then wipe it off evenly. Otherwise, strip with lacquer thinner, acetone or paint stripper and restain smaller parts at a time (or get a second person to help).
- The color of the stain doesn't match what you expected from the name on the label. Names are simply manufacturer's interpretations. There are no industry standards. One manufacturer's "mahogany" may differ from another manufacturer's "mahogany," for example.
- The color of the stain on your project isn't the same as on the color sample in the store. Woods color differently. Always try the stain on scrap from your project, sanded to the same grit sandpaper, and make adjustments (add pigment, thinner or mix with another color stain) if necessary to get what you want.
- Glue from squeeze-out or fingerprints seals the wood preventing stain penetration. Sand or scrape off the glue through the stain and restain that area, or leave the splotch and disguise it by painting in the correct coloring after you have applied a coat of finish.

Stain problems such as blotching and getting the color wrong can be extremely difficult to fix. You can usually remove some of the color by wiping with the thinner for the stain. If the stain contains a binder (it isn't simply dye), you can use a paint stripper. But nothing short of sanding will remove all the color.

## CONDITIONING THE WOOD

The purpose of "conditioning" or "washcoating" wood before applying a stain is to reduce blotching, which is uneven coloring caused by varying densities in the wood. A wood conditioner (also called "stain controller") or washcoat is any finish thinned to about 10% solids so it doesn't fully "seal" the wood. Some of the stain can still penetrate.

The woods that blotch are softwoods such as pine, and tight-grain hardwoods such as maple, birch and cherry. There's no point in applying a wood conditioner/washcoat to medium- or coarse-grain woods such as walnut, mahogany or oak.

Varnish wood conditioners (the common ones found in home centers and paint stores) are varnish thinned with about two parts mineral spirits (paint thinner). You can make your own. The key to getting the wood conditioner to work is to let it dry fully before applying the stain — at least six hours, better overnight.

# Understanding Finishes

## Finishes and Finishing

### DEFINITION

A wood finish is a clear, transparent coating applied to wood to protect it from moisture and to make it look richer and deeper. This differs from paint, which is a wood finish loaded with enough pigment to hide the wood. And it differs from a stain, which is a wood finish and a colorant (pigment or dye) with a lot of thinner added so the excess stain is easy to wipe off. The remainder just colors the wood; it doesn't hide the wood.

A stain can also be a thinned dye with no wood finish added.

### ANOTHER DEFINITION

The term "finish" can also refer to the entire built-up coating, which could consist of stain, several coats of finish (a "coat" is one application layer) and maybe some coloring steps in between these coats. For some reason, we have only one word to refer both to the clear coating used, and to all the steps used.

Usually, the context makes clear which is being referred to.

### PURPOSE OF A FINISH

A finish serves two purposes: protection and decoration.

Protection means resistance to moisture penetration. In all cases, the thicker the finish the more moisture resistant it is. Three coats are more protective than two, for example. Boiled linseed oil, 100% tung oil and wax dry soft and gummy, so all the excess has to be wiped off after each application to achieve a functional surface. Therefore, no significant thickness or protection can be achieved.

Finishes decorate wood by making it look richer and deeper. The impact is less on unstained lighter woods such as maple and birch, and greater on stained and darker woods such as cherry and walnut.

### TYPES OF WOOD FINISHES

- Oil (boiled linseed oil, 100% tung oil and blends of these oils and varnish);
- Oil-based varnish (including alkyd, polyurethane, spar, wiping and gel varnish);
- Water-based finish (a finish that thins and cleans up with water);
- Shellac (an ancient finish derived from resin secretions of the lac bug);
- Lacquer (the finish used on almost all household furniture made since the 1920s); and
- A large number of two-part, high-performance finishes used in industry and by many professional cabinet shops.

### PRIMARY DIFFERENCES AMONG THE TYPES

**Scratch, solvent and heat resistance.**
- Oil-based varnishes and high-performance finishes provide the best scratch, solvent and heat resistance.
- Water-based finishes are next.
- Shellac and lacquer are susceptible to all three types of damage.
- Oil is too thin to be effective.

**Color.**
- Water-based finishes add no color to the wood and don't darken as they age.
- All the other finishes add some degree of yellow-to-orange coloring and continue to darken a little as they age.

Three types of coatings: Top; just clear finish, middle; paint, bottom; stain. The bands separating the sections are left uncoated, for comparison.

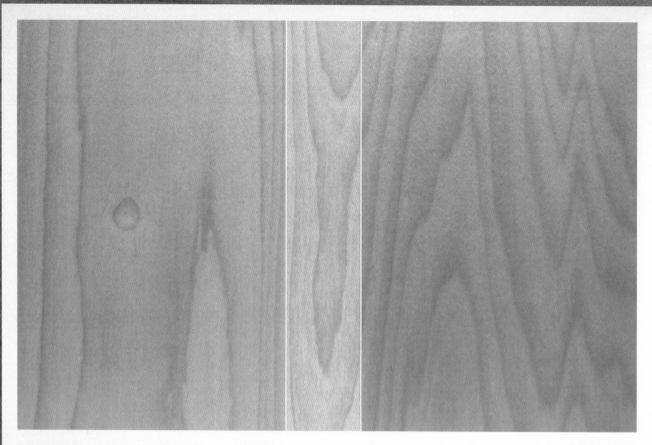

The left section of this panel was finished with water-based polyure-thane, which, like all water-based finishes, adds no color to the wood. The finish just makes the wood a little darker (compared to the lighter strip down the middle, which was covered with tape). The right section was finished with oil-based polyurethane, which, like all finishes except water-based finishes adds some degree of yellow/orange coloring to the wood. Oil-based polyurethane continues to darken as it ages, while water-based polyurethane doesn't darken anymore.

**Drying time.**

- Shellac, lacquer and high-performance finishes dry the fastest.
- Water-based finishes are next.
- Varnish and oil require overnight drying in a warm room.

**Solvent safety.**

- Boiled linseed oil and 100% tung oil are the least toxic finishes to breathe during application because they don't contain solvent.
- Water-based finishes (thinned with water and a little solvent) and shellac (thinned with denatured alcohol) are next.
- Oil-based varnish thins with mineral spirits (paint thinner), which some people find objectionable but which isn't especially toxic.
- Lacquer and high-performance finishes thin with solvents that are the most toxic to be around.

## SEALING WOOD

The first coat of any finish seals the wood—that is, stops up the pores in the wood so the next coat of finish (or other liquids) don't penetrate easily. This first coat raises the grain of the wood making it feel rough. You should sand this first coat (with just your hand backing the sandpaper) to make it feel smooth. You don't need a special product for this first coat unless you have one of two problems you want to overcome.

- Alkyd varnish and lacquer gum up sandpaper when sanded, so manu-facturers of each provide a special product called "sanding sealer" with dry lubricants added to make sand-ing easier and speed your work. Sanding sealers weaken the finish, however, so you should use them only when you're finishing a large project or doing production work.
- Sometimes, there are problems in the wood that have to be blocked off with a special sealer so they don't telegraph through all the coats. These problems are resinous knots in softwoods such as pine, silicone oil from furniture polishes that causes the finish to bunch up into ridges or hollow out into craters, and smoke and animal-urine odors. The finish that blocks these problems ("seals them in") is shellac and should be used for the first coat. Notice that, except for resinous knots, the prob-lems occur only in refinishing.

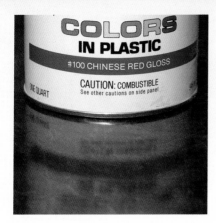

A finish can have an infinite number of sheens depending on how much flatting agent is added. Here are three typical examples: from left to right—gloss, semi-gloss and satin.

## SHEEN

Oil-based varnishes, water-based finishes and lacquers are available in a variety of sheens, ranging from gloss to flat. All sheens other than gloss are created by the solid-particle "flatting agents" manufacturers add to the finish. The more flatting agent added the flatter the sheen. These flatting particles settle to the bottom of the can, so you have to stir them into suspension before each use.

## FINISH APPLICATION

Oil, wax, wiping varnish and gel varnish can be applied with a cloth or brush, then wiped off. The other finishes are applied with a brush or spray gun.

Brushing is very intuitive — essentially no different than brushing paint. Spraying is also intuitive, but spray-gun care and tuning is more complicated, and spray guns and their sources of air (compressor or turbine) are considerably more expensive than brushes.

## APPLICATION PROBLEMS

Common problems and ways to avoid them:

- Brush marks. Eliminate these by thinning the finish 10% to 30% so it levels better.
- Runs and sags. Watch what is happening in a reflected light and brush out the runs and sags as they occur.
- Dust nibs. Keep your tools, the finish and the air in the room as clean as possible.
- Bubbles. Brush back over to pop the bubbles, or thin the finish 10% to 30% so the bubbles have more time to pop out.

No matter what the problem, you can always fix it by sanding the finish level and applying another coat.

You can get any sheen you want by pouring off some of the gloss from a can in which the flatting agent has settled (don't let the store clerk shake the can) and blending the two parts. Or you can mix cans of gloss and satin to get something in between. You will need to apply the finish to see the sheen you'll get after the finish dries. It's the last coat you apply that determines the sheen (there is no cumulative effect), so you can experiment with each coat.

# Preparing Wood for a Finish

The reason you have to sand wood before applying a finish is to remove machine marks. All machine tools leave cuts or impressions in wood that are highlighted by stains and finishes — especially by stains. Before machine tools came into use in the mid-nineteenth century no sanding was needed. Indeed, there was no sandpaper. Wood was smoothed with hand planes and scrapers.

You can still use hand tools to smooth wood, but few people choose this route because machine tools are much faster and easier to learn to use. The price, then, for using machine tools alone for smoothing and shaping wood is that you have to finish off with sandpaper to take out the machine marks.

It helps to remind yourself of this. Sanding is the price you pay for the increased efficiency of substituting machine tools for hand tools.

## RULES FOR SANDING WOOD

Here are some general considerations for sanding wood.

• Always sand in the direction of the wood grain (from end-to-end of the board) when possible. Sanding cross-grain (across the board) or diagonally to the grain tears the wood fibers, leaving more obvious scratches that then require more work to sand out.

• Always begin sanding with a grit sandpaper that cuts through the problem (machine marks, gouges, scratches, etc.) efficiently and removes it ENTIRELY without creating larger than necessary scratches that then have to be sanded out. Then sand out the scratches left by this grit sandpaper with a finer-grit sandpaper and continue with finer

With a stain applied you can clearly see the cuts and impressions left by the machine. These have to be sanded out to get a good final result.

Sandpaper is measured by the size of the grit that is glued to the paper. The lower the number the coarser, or larger, the grit size. The higher the number the finer the scratches. Typical sandpaper grits used for sanding wood are #80, #100, #120, #150, #180 and #220.

and finer grits until you reach the scratch size that doesn't show under a stain or finish. Stain highlights scratches much more than a clear, transparent finish. So you don't have to sand to as fine a grit if you aren't applying a stain.

• You can sand progressively through each higher-numbered grit, or you can skip grits if you sand a little longer with each to remove the larger scratches.

• Typically on machined wood, you would begin sanding with #80 or #100 grit, whichever works most efficiently — that is, removes the problem in four or five overlapping passes without leaving larger-than-necessary scratches.

• On factory-sanded, veneered plywood or MDF, you would typically begin sanding with #120, or even #150 grit if there aren't any scratches.

• If you can create an even scratch pattern lined up with the grain of the wood using #150-grit sandpaper, you may not have to sand finer. But in the beginning, I recommend you always sand at least to #180 grit.

• Random-orbit and vibrator sanders leave cross-grain swirls in the wood. You have to sand fine enough so these swirls don't show under a finish or a stain and finish. This usually means sanding at least to #220-grit. But the better procedure is to sand to #180 grit and then sand by hand in the direction of the grain with #180 grit to remove the swirl marks. On flat surfaces, back the sandpaper with a flat sanding block.

**1** When sanding flat surfaces, always back the sandpaper with a flat block so you don't gouge into the softer parts of the wood with your fingers.

**2** On non-flat surfaces, such as the bevel on this raised-panel door, fold the sandpaper and sand with just your hand backing the sandpaper.

**3** The most efficient hand-held machine tool for sanding is a random-orbit sander. This sander is better at disguising swirl marks than a vibrator sander because of the randomness of its movement. With both of these sanders, use a light touch. Pressing leaves deeper and more obvious swirl cuts in the wood. These then have to be sanded out. Move the sander slowly over the surface of the wood in a pattern that covers all areas approximately equally. You could sand up to a grit sandpaper that doesn't leave visible swirl marks in the wood, but it's easier to sand out the swirl marks by hand after sanding to #180 or #220 grit. Always sand in the direction of the wood grain.

# TIP: Wood Putty

It's always best to avoid having to use wood putty to fill gouges or cracks. Wood putty in cracks will probably come out in time. And wood putty anywhere usually shows because it doesn't take stain the same as the surrounding wood. Wood putty is simple to use. Just press it into the recess and scrape off the excess with the putty knife. Let it dry, which it will do quickly unless the recess is deep, then sand the area smooth.

**4** Even without pressing, random orbit sanders leave swirl marks that have to be sanded out to get a good result. The best procedure is to sand by hand in the direction of the wood grain to remove them. It doesn't take much.

**5** The biggest problem for beginners is knowing how much to sand. Here's a trick you can use when sanding with the coarsest-grit sandpaper. Draw some pencil marks on the wood, then sand until these marks are gone. You could even do this a second time to be sure. Don't draw the pencil marks with the finer grit sandpapers, just with the coarsest grit you begin with. Very little sanding is needed with the finer grits to remove the scratches from the coarser grits. It's most efficient to sand out all the problems with just the coarsest grit you begin with.

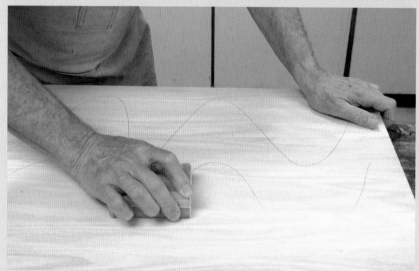

**6** Pay special attention to the ends of flat panels. A trick you can use to be sure you've sanded enough near these ends is to sand with short strokes once or twice across the surface. Then sand lengthways all the way to both edges.

**7** Machined boards have sharp edges. A finish won't hold well to these edges. You should soften them with a quick pass or two with medium-grit sandpaper. Sand just enough so the edges don't feel sharp anymore.

**8** The most efficient tool for dusting is a vacuum. Use it between sanding grits to remove the dust before moving to the next grit and at the end to remove the dust before staining or finishing.

**9** You can also use a dust brush for dusting. But it kicks dust into the air, and the dust will settle for quite some time. This will force you to postpone moving to the finishing steps for a while.

## SANDING WOOD

You can sand by hand or use a hand-held sanding machine. Though sanding by hand is more work, it is more efficient. You can remove more wood faster.

## SANDPAPER

I've always liked sanding by hand rather than with a hand-held sanding machine. Sanding by hand is faster, and there are no swirl marks to contend with, though there is an issue with perspiration. If you drip on the wood and you intend to stain it, sand it very well, or wet the entire part with water and sand it well. Raised grain from a drip will stain darker. Here's the system I've developed for using sandpaper efficiently.

**1** (ABOVE RIGHT) Fold a standard 9" x 11" sheet of sandpaper into thirds across the width so that each third is about 3⅝" across.

**2** (RIGHT) Crimp the sandpaper with your thumb and index finger.

**3** Fold the sandpaper back on itself and crimp again.

**4** Tear the sandpaper along the crimped edge. You could also tear off 1/3 of a sheet over the sharp edge of a tabletop. It's not a good idea to use a knife or scissors to cut the sandpaper because it will quickly dull the tool.

**5** Here's the 1/3 sheet you're going to use for sanding.

**6** To use the 1/3 sheet with a sanding block, fold it in half lengthways and wrap it around the bottom side of a sanding block as shown. Use your fingers to hold the edge with the two flaps and your thumb to hold the folded edge. The edge with the two flaps will be the only part of the sandpaper that will be wasted, so minimize the amount that is wrapped around the block — just enough so you can get a good grip. When you have worn this side of the folded sandpaper, flip it and sand with the other side.

**7** After sanding with both sides of the folded ¹⁄₃ sheet, open up the sandpaper and wrap it around the sanding block so you can use the middle part.

**8** The sanding block I'm using is home-made. It makes much more efficient use of the sandpaper than any commercial sanding block I've come across. My sanding block measures 3⁷⁄₈" x 2³⁄₄" and is about 1¹⁄₄" thick, with the top edges rounded over. It has ¹⁄₈" gasket cork glued to the bottom to create a softer base. You can buy the cork at an auto-parts store or at many craft stores. Use wood glue and clamp the cork to the block while the glue dries. Instead of making a sanding block, you can use a widely available "sanding sponge." It won't last as long, but it is exactly the same size.

**9** To use the ¹⁄₃ sheet for sanding with only your hand backing the sandpaper, fold the sheet in thirds. By flipping and re-folding the sandpaper, you can use all three sides and gain the benefit of significantly reduced slippage because of the gritted flap in the center.

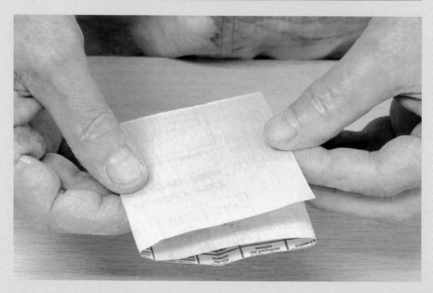

## GLUE SPLOTCHES

It's rare that you can build an entire project without getting some glue on the surface, either seepage from joints or from glue on your hands.

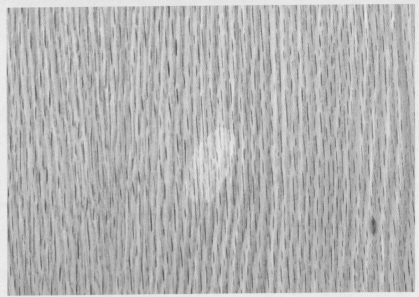

**1** A glue splotch may not show up much under a transparent finish, but it always shows under a stain. Here's a common situation where glue seeped from the joint on a panel door. The glue wasn't caught until after the stain and finish were applied.

**2** The easy way to find areas with unwanted glue on the surface is to wet it. To avoid having to sand raised grain caused by water, use mineral spirits (paint thinner) to wet the surface. It will soak deeper into the wood than the glue did, making the wood darker. The areas with glue will then show up lighter.

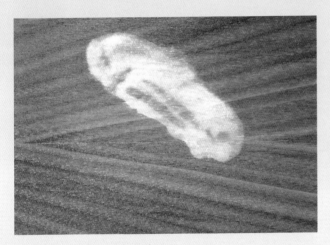

**3** Once you find the areas with glue, you have to remove it. The best method is to sand or scrape the glue off the wood. You can also soften the glue enough with water, turning the glue white, so it's easy to scrub off. If you use water, you should wet the entire surface and sand it smooth so the wood stains evenly. Raised grain will stain darker. A third method of removing unwanted glue is with xylene, the active ingredient in the commercial products "Oops!" and "Goof Off." You can use any of these to soften the glue so it can be scrubbed off, using a toothbrush or soft wire brush to scrub in the grain of coarse- and medium-grain woods. Xylene doesn't raise the wood grain.

**4** Another solution to glue splotches is to "paint" them after at least one coat of finish. This is probably the best course of action if you don't catch the problem before staining. The usual procedure is to paint the grain first, connecting to the wood at each end, then color in the rest. Pulling this off can be tricky, however, because it requires a good sense of color. You could also sand out the glue splotch before you apply the finish, then restain. Sand the entire part so the restaining will be even. Sand to the finest grit you used to sand the wood. You don't need to remove all the color, just make it fairly even. If the part doesn't restain dark enough, apply more stain and sand it wet with sandpaper one grit coarser. Then wipe off the excess stain.

# Stripping Old Finish and Paint

Paints and finishes deteriorate as they age. First they become dull, then they start to crack and craze. When they reach this stage, they no longer perform their protective role of keeping moisture from getting into the wood, and they may also look bad. In the case of furniture, a deteriorated finish should be removed and replaced. Paint often can be cleaned and painted over.

There are two ways to remove a finish from furniture: sand it off, or strip it off. It's not wise to use a heat gun on furniture because the heat may cause veneer to delaminate or scorch the wood.

Sanding is also damaging and can lead to difficult coloring problems because you can't help but sand unevenly through stain or patina (the natural color changes that occur in wood as it ages). Only if the finish is flaking and comes off easily should you sand it off.

Though it's messy, the best method of removing an old finish or paint is with a paint-and-varnish remover, also called "stripper" or "paint stripper."

Despite the message of the Antiques Roadshow, it's extremely rare that you

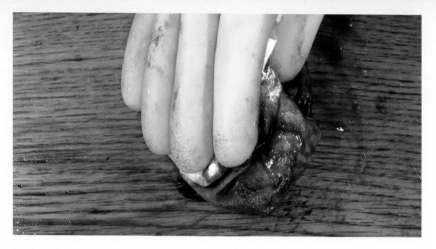

Shellac and lacquer, the finishes used on almost all household furniture for the last 200 years, dissolve when paint stripper is applied.

would come across furniture that is more valuable with its old deteriorated finish left intact. Refinishing saves old furniture; it doesn't destroy value.

## HOW STRIPPERS WORK

Paint strippers consist of a solvent or combination of solvents strong enough to penetrate a paint or finish film. These solvents act on the film in one of three ways depending on what is being stripped.

- They dissolve the film into a gunk that can be wiped off.
- They swell the film so it blisters and can be scraped off.
- They break the bond of the film to the wood so the film can be lifted off in sheets with a putty knife.

Most old finishes (shellac and lacquer) dissolve. Paint and varnish swell and blister. Many of the newer high-performance finishes hold together but lose their attachment to the wood.

Paint and most varnishes blister when paint stripper is applied.

High performance finishes, often used on office furniture and kitchen cabinets during the last 40 years, lift off in sheets when paint stripper is applied.

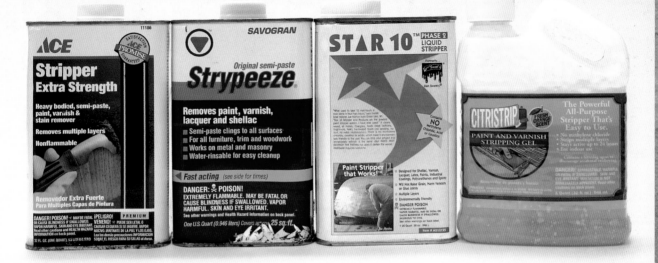

## CHOOSING A PAINT STRIPPER

There are four categories of paint strippers. Within each category, there's not much difference. But there are significant differences among the categories. It's important to understand these differences and how to identify each.

Methylene chloride (MC) is the strongest and fastest-acting stripping solvent we have available to us. It is also a very heavy solvent, and it is non-flammable. So cans of strippers that contain the most methylene chloride are noticeably heavier than other strippers, and they have "non-flammable" written somewhere on the label.

Next in order of strength and speed are strippers with some methylene chloride together with a number of other solvents. Because of the other solvents, these strippers are flammable. So to identify them, look for "flammable" on the label and "methylene chloride" listed as an ingredient.

Third in line for strength and speed are strippers that contain a number of solvents similar to those in weak MC but no methylene chloride. These strippers are therefore flammable and don't have methylene chloride listed as an ingredient.

Each of these three strippers evaporates very rapidly. So to keep them wet

longer, wax is included in the stripper. It rises to the surface of the brushed stripper and forms a mild barrier to evaporation. If you brush back over the stripper, you break through this wax barrier and allow the solvents to evaporate — until the wax barrier reforms.

This is the reason for the common instruction to brush in one direction only. You can of course brush in both directions. But brush as little as possible.

The wax is a real problem. Some of it remains in the wood after you have removed all the paint or finish, and the wax can interfere with the drying and bonding of a new finish. It's important that you wash off this wax residue with a solvent: mineral spirits, naphtha, denatured alcohol, lacquer thinner or acetone.

Wash the wood with a soaking wet cloth, then dry off the wetness. Do this several times to be sure you have removed all the wax.

The fourth category of paint stripper is n-methyl pyrrolidone (NMP). It evaporates very slowly. It's also the most expensive of all the solvents used. So other solvents, usually esters, are added to reduce the cost. You can identify this stripper easily by the packaging, plastic rather than metal containers.

NMP isn't as strong as the other solvents but it evaporates so slowly that it

The four categories of paint strippers from left to right are strong methylene chloride (MC), weak methylene chloride (MC), non-methylene chloride (MC) and n-methyl pyrrolidone (NMP).

can remain in contact with the coating for days as long as you apply it thickly. If you aren't in a hurry, this stripper actually requires less work.

All four of these strippers are widely available in a fairly thick consistency, usually called "semi-paste." So the stripper clings well to vertical surfaces. This is the consistency you should use unless you are soaking parts.

All four strippers are also unhealthy to be around, so you should always work outside in the shade or arrange an air flow — in one window or door and out another.

All four strippers will also work on virtually every type of coating if kept wet long enough. So make your choice based on price and how fast you want the stripper to work. Practically speaking, it's usually best to use either a strong MC or NMP stripper (allowing a day or two for NMP) on paint, varnish and high-performance coatings.

## WHAT YOU NEED

(The following items are all available from a home center, paint store or woodworking store or catalog/website.)

- Paint stripper.
- Metal can to work from.
- Solvents such as denatured alcohol and paint thinner.
- Lint-free rags such as old T-shirts and/or heavy-duty paper towels.
- Butyl or neoprene, solvent-resistant work gloves.
- Wide putty knife.
- Two-inch, or wider old or inexpensive, nautral-brush paintbrush.
- Coarse #1 steel wool and/or abrasive scrub pad.
- #180-grit sandpaper.

**1** The first step is to disassemble the object to be stripped.

**2** Brush the stripper thick onto the wood. Brush back and forth as little as possible to minimize solvent evaporation.

## STEPS FOR USING PAINT STRIPPERS

1. Disassemble the object to be stripped, making the stripping easier. Remove hardware and soak it in a coffee can with stripper if it needs stripping.

2. Work outdoors in the shade or in a room where you have arranged cross-ventilation provided by fans — air in from one door or window and out another. Ideal temperature should be in the 70s. Hotter and the evaporation is faster; colder and the stripping action slows significantly. Don't work near an open flame or source of sparks if you're using a flammable stripper.

3. Wear eye protection and solvent-resistant gloves (butyl or neoprene).

4. Spread newspapers on the ground or floor to catch the waste.

5. Shake the container of stripper, then cover it with a cloth and open the cap slowly to allow the pressure inside to escape. Pour the stripper into a large can, such as a coffee can.

6. Brush the stripper onto the wood using an old or inexpensive paintbrush. Avoid unnecessary brushing; you want to lay on a thick coat, but also minimize solvent evaporation. (Be aware that some synthetic bristles will dissolve in methylene-chloride strippers.)

7. Allow the stripper time to work. Test the paint or finish occasionally with a putty knife to see if you can lift it from the wood. Apply more stripper as the original dries out. All strippers will lift many layers of paint or finish at once if the surface is kept wet so the stripper has time to penetrate.

8. Remove the dissolved, blistered or softened paint or finish using one or more of the following methods. Use paper towels to soak up and wipe off dissolved finish. Scrape the "gunk" off flat surfaces into a can or cardboard box with a plastic spreader or wide, dull putty knife (round its edges so it doesn't

**3** If the stripper has dissolved the coating, simply wipe it off. You can use heavy-duty paper towels instead of cloth rags.

**4** On flat surfaces, it's faster and less messy to scrape off most of the dissolved finish into a cardboard box before wiping with a cloth or towel.

**5** Blistered paint is easy to scrape off.

No matter how you get the paint or finish off the wood, if you're using anything but n-methyl pyrrolidone, wash the wood several times with solvent to get rid of the wax residue. With NMP strippers, you can wash with denatured alcohol to dry off the slow evaporating NMP.

scratch). Break blistered or softened film loose from moldings, turnings and carvings with #1 steel wool or an abrasive pad. Pull a coarse string or hemp rope around the recesses of turnings to work out blistered paint or finish. Pick softened paint or finish out of cracks and recesses with sharpened sticks or dowels, which won't damage the wood as metal picks will.

9. Wash the wood with mineral spirits, naphtha, denatured alcohol, lacquer thinner or acetone to remove wax residue left from strippers containing wax (the ones in metal cans). You can wash with a hose instead if the strip-

per is "water-washable," which means that it contains a detergent. But, be aware that this will raise the grain of the wood forcing you to do some fairly heavy sanding.

10. Let the solvent evaporate out of the stripping sludge, then dispose of it in the trash unless local laws forbid this. (The dried sludge is what was on the furniture before your stripped it, so it is no more polluting than tossing the entire painted or finished object in the trash.)

11. If you used an NMP stripper and you want to begin applying a stain or finish within a few days, wash the surface of the wood with denatured al-

cohol to remove residue NMP solvent, which evaporates extremely slowly.

12. Finish by sanding the dried wood lightly with #180-grit sandpaper to ensure that you have removed all the finish. The wood should powder, not clog the sandpaper. There's no reason to sand heavily unless there's something you want to remove. There's also no reason to use a flat block to back your sandpaper unless you're sanding heavily.

## USE ALCOHOL OR LACQUER THINNER

Instead of using a paint stripper to remove a finish, you can use denatured alcohol or lacquer thinner if the finish is shellac or lacquer. The advantage is that you don't have to deal with removing the residue wax.

Determine if the finish is shellac or lacquer by dabbing some denatured alcohol or lacquer thinner onto the finish with your finger (photo at right). If the finish gets sticky and dissolves with denatured alcohol, the finish is shellac. If the finish gets sticky and dissolves with lacquer thinner, the finish is lacquer. If nothing happens, the finish is something else and you will have to use a paint stripper. In this photo the finish is shellac.

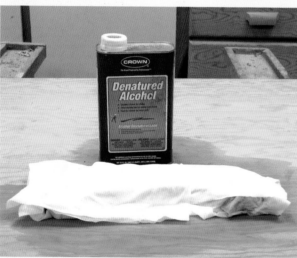

(ABOVE LEFT) Soak some rags or heavy-duty paper towels with denatured alcohol and lay them out on the part or wrap them around the part. Keep the rags wet. Check every few minutes until the finish liquefies.

(ABOVE RIGHT) When the finish liquefies, simply wipe it off with the soaked rags. Then dry the wood with a dry cloth or paper towel.

## Keys to Identifying Each of the Four Categories of Strippers

|  | STRONG MC | WEAK MC | NON MC | NMP |
|---|---|---|---|---|
| PACKAGING | Metal | Metal | Metal | Plastic |
| CONTAINS MC | Yes | Yes | No | No |
| FLAMMABILITY | No | Yes | Yes | No |
| WEIGHT | Heavier | Average | Average | Average |
| EXPENSE | 2nd expensive | 3rd expensive | Least | Most |

# Common Stripping Problems

Here are some of the most common problems you will run into stripping furniture and what to do about them.

## THE STRIPPER DOESN'T WORK

If the stripper you're using doesn't dissolve, blister, or break the bond of the paint or finish film from the wood, either you need to allow more time for the stripper to work or use a stronger stripper.

First allow more time. Strippers work much slower in temperatures below 65 degrees. Keep the surface wet by applying additional coats of stripper or covering the surface with plastic wrap to prevent evaporation.

If you still have problems, try a stronger stripper. The only paint or finish that can't be removed with a solvent-based stripper is milk paint. It was used in the 18th century and in rural areas of the U.S. in the 19th century. You can remove it with lye.

Some modern high-performance coatings are very difficult to strip. Rough them up with coarse sandpaper to increase the surface area, then try again with a strong methylene-chloride stripper.

## YOU CAN'T GET PAINT OUT OF THE PORES

Paint is softened by the stripper but doesn't come out of the pores until some mechanical force is applied. Stripping shops often use a pressure washer. You can use that (with a water-washable stripper) or a soft brass-wire brush, which won't damage hardwoods.

Apply more stripper to the surface, then scrub in the direction of the grain. Remove the gunk with rags or paper towels. Repeat until the wood is clean.

## YOU CAN'T GET STAIN OUT

There are several types of stain, and whether a stripper removes the stain depends on how that particular stain is affected by the stripper. If the stripper doesn't remove the stain, use household bleach to remove dye stains, or scrub the wood with a brass-wire brush together with more stripper to remove pigment stains.

You don't have to remove stain, however, if you intend to restain darker than the color of the stripped wood. Simply restain right over the remaining color.

You can tell that all the finish is off when there aren't any remaining shiny places on the wood or in the pores when the wood is dry. You can also test by sanding lightly with fine-grit sandpaper after the wood is dry. If the sandpaper clogs, the finish hasn't been entirely removed.

## STRIPPER STREAKS AND DARKENS THE WOOD

Lye and any stripper containing an alkali may darken wood. The darkening often shows up as streaks resembling brush marks. To bleach out the dark stains, make a saturated solution of oxalic-acid crystals, available at pharmacies and many paint stores. Use hot water.

Brush the solution over the entire surface, not just over the stains. Let the oxalic acid dry back into crystal form. Then wash the crystals off the wood with a hose or well-soaked sponge or cloth. The crystals will cause an uncontrollable coughing if you brush them into the air and breathe them.

Oxalic acid will also remove black water rings and rust stains. It has little effect on the natural color of the wood.

## SANDPAPER CLOGS AFTER STRIPPING

Clogged sandpaper indicates that some finish remains on the wood, or that the stripper hasn't completely evaporated. As long as all the finish has been removed, sanding isn't necessary if the wood is smooth. Sanding will remove the wood's patina (the appearance of age brought about by light and use).

## WOOD WON'T STAIN EVENLY

You may not have removed all the old finish. If this is the case, you'll have to resume stripping until all the finish is removed. Uneven stain penetration can also be caused by uneven density or swirly grain in the wood itself.

## FINISH WON'T DRY, OR PEELS AFTER CURING

Both of these problems are caused by wax left on the wood by the stripper. All strippers other than NMP contain wax. The wood must be washed thoroughly (not neutralized as most directions suggest) with a detergent or solvent for wax. Flood the surface, then wipe with a dry cloth, turning it frequently so you lift the wax from the wood rather than just move it around.

# Wiping Varnish

Wiping varnish is the finish I recommend you use if you are finishing for the first time. Wiping varnish is a term I coined in 1990 to categorize a large number of very popular finishes that are sold individually under many different names but are actually all the same — oil-based alkyd or polyurethane varnish thinned about half with mineral spirits (paint thinner). Collecting them into a category removes the mystique manufacturers attempt to create and makes the finish easier to understand. It also allows us to discuss uniform application procedures that apply to all brands.

Notice from the pictures that many of the brands of wiping varnish are labeled "tung oil," "tung oil varnish" or "tung oil finish." None of these are tung oil and few have any tung oil in them. Even in the rare cases when a little tung oil is added, it is insignificant and doesn't justify the misleading naming. All of these products are simply oil-based alkyd or polyurethane varnish thinned about half with mineral spirits. (The wiping varnish, Waterlox, is a phenolic varnish.)

The difference between varnish and oil finishes is that varnish dries hard so it can be built up on the wood for better moisture resistance. Oil (boiled linseed oil, 100% tung oil and blends of oil and varnish) dries soft so all the excess has to be wiped off after each coat. No built-up moisture resistance can be achieved. This is a really big difference!

You can distinguish wiping varnish labeled "tung oil" from real tung oil by

These are typical commercial brands of wiping varnish sold in home centers and paint stores.

These are typical commercial brands of wiping varnish sold in woodworking stores and catalogs.

the following: real tung oil is always labeled "100% tung oil," so far as I know; no brands of real tung oil contain thinner (mineral spirits — usually called "petroleum distillates" or "aliphatic hydrocarbons" on the label); wiping varnish always contains thinner.

For this exercise/project you will make your own wiping varnish, though you could, of course, use a commercial brand. Making your own gives you more control because you can add more or less thinner.

## Wiping Varnish;
## Difficulty: Low.

### WHAT IS IT?

Any brand of oil-based alkyd (regular) varnish or oil-based polyurethane varnish in any sheen (gloss or satin) thinned about half with mineral spirits (paint thinner).

### RULES FOR APPLICATION

- Wipe or brush on the wood and
- Wipe off all the excess; or
- Brush off some or most of the excess using a "dry" brush; or
- Leave all the excess (only on flat, horizontal surfaces).
- Allow to dry overnight or at least 6 hours in a warm room, garage or shop.
- Sand each dried coat lightly with #320- or #400-grit sandpaper to remove dust nibs before applying the next coat.
- Three or four coats are usually minimum for good results.

### WHEN TO USE

On any object — furniture, trim, cabinets — or even floors when you want a protective and durable finish that is easy to apply and produces almost perfect results.

### COMPATIBILITY

Can be used over any stain or finish, as long as it is dry, clean and dull. Also, any finish can be applied over wiping varnish as long as it is dry, clean and dull. If you spray lacquer, however, spray light coats because the lacquer thinner could cause the varnish to blister.

### ADVANTAGES

- Very easy to apply.
- Very protective and durable after several coats.
- Easy to get an almost flawless result.
- Adds warmth to dark and dark-stained woods.

Because of the uninformative naming, you need a method for identifying commercial wiping varnishes. Unfortunately, you can rarely do this from the label. You will need to put a puddle of the finish on the lid or other non-porous surface and see how it cures. If the product thins and cleans up with mineral spirits and isn't labeled "varnish" or "polyurethane," and it cures hard and smooth after several days in a warm room, it's wiping varnish.

### DISADVANTAGES

- Takes many more coats to achieve the same thickness and protection as fewer coats of brushed-on alkyd or polyurethane varnish.
- Adds a noticeable yellow/orange coloring to light-colored woods.
- Can result in streaking when using a satin wiping varnish.

### COMMON APPLICATION PROBLEMS

- Dust nibs, especially if the finish room is dusty.
- Runs on vertical surfaces if most of the excess isn't wiped or brushed off.

### MAKE YOUR OWN

- One part gloss, oil-based polyurethane varnish; one part mineral spirits (paint thinner).

### VARIATIONS

- Higher percentage of polyurethane varnish to achieve a faster build.
- Higher percentage of mineral spirits to achieve a longer working time and better leveling.
- Substitute any other oil-based varnish.

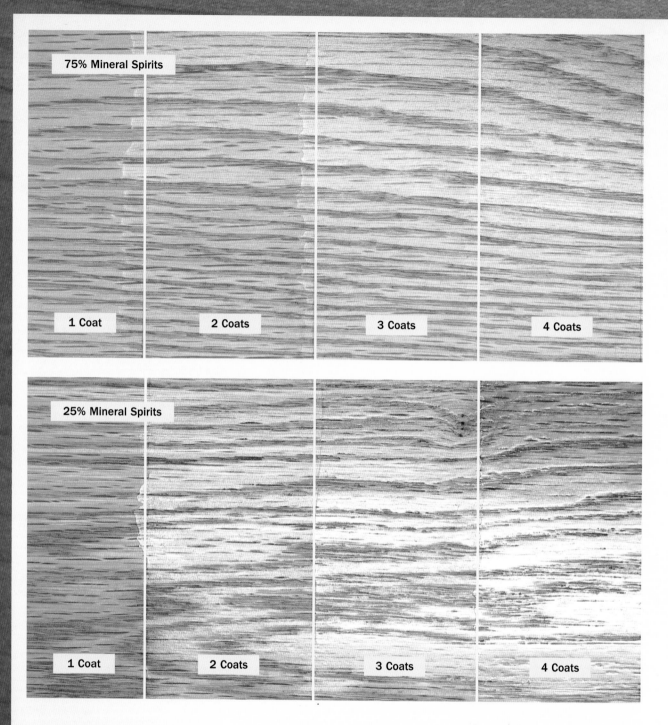

75% Mineral Spirits

1 Coat     2 Coats     3 Coats     4 Coats

25% Mineral Spirits

1 Coat     2 Coats     3 Coats     4 Coats

You have much more control of the rate of build per coat if you make your own wiping varnish than if you buy a commercial brand. The top panel (above) was finished with 1, 2, 3, and 4 coats of polyurethane thinned with 75% mineral spirits — that is, a one-part polyurethane to three parts thinner.

The bottom panel was finished with 1, 2, 3, and 4 coats of polyurethane thinned with 25% mineral spirits — that is, three parts polyurethane to one-part thinner. In both cases, the finish was brushed and left. You can clearly see the faster build using the three-to-one mix. Though I'm going to use a half-

and-half blend in this exercise/project, similar to commercial brands, I recommend you try the three-to-one mix because it is still thin enough to be easy to apply, and it builds faster. You can always add some more mineral spirits if the finish is tacking up too quickly.

## WHAT YOU NEED

- A 16" × 24" or larger sheet of ½" or ¾" veneered plywood or MDF. Any hardwood veneer is OK. (From your scraps, a wood supplier or from one of many cabinet shops that often throw away pieces this size.)

(The following items are all available from a home center, paint store or woodworking store or catalog/website.)

- A pint or quart of gloss, oil-based polyurethane varnish.
- A pint or quart of mineral spirits.
- A clean plastic container, coffee can or wide-mouth jar with a lid. (Also from your kitchen.)
- Latex or other type of protective gloves.
- Lint-free rags such as old, clean T-shirts, cheesecloth or "Scott rags," which are soft white paper towels in box or roll sold to painters.

- A good quality natural-bristle brush (best), or foam brush, or an inexpensive "chip" brush. A width of 2" is easy to use on most projects.

- A sheet each of #320- or #400-grit sandpaper.
- A small brown paper bag. (Also from the supermarket.)

## MAKE YOUR OWN

Instead of buying a poorly labeled wiping varnish at the store and taking the risk that you get something else — for example, an oil/varnish blend — just make your own. All you have to do is thin any full strength, oil-based varnish or polyurethane a quarter-to-a-half with mineral spirits.

To make your own wiping varnish for this exercise/project, pour approximately equal amounts of oil-based, gloss polyurethane and mineral spirits into a clean wide-mouth container.

Stir the thinned polyurethane or the two parts will remain separated.

Wipe-off Excess Method
1  2  3  4  5  6

Dry Brush Excess Method
1  2  3  4  5  6

Leave Excess Method
1  2  3  4  5  6

## APPLYING WIPING VARNISH

I'm going to show you three methods of applying wiping varnish: wipe off the excess; "dry-brush" the excess; and leave the excess. You can use any of the methods for all the coats or alternate among them. I suggest you try both of the first two methods to see which you like best. You can use the third method on flat, horizontal surfaces.

Here are pictures of one through six coats using each application method. In the upper picture I applied from one to six coats and wiped off the excess after each. In the middle picture I applied from one to six coats and dry-brushed the excess after each. In the lower picture I applied from one to six coats and left them to dry. You can see that wiping off produces the slowest build and leaving produces the fastest build.

## WIPE OFF EXCESS METHOD

Brush or wipe the wiping varnish onto the wood and wipe off the excess. This method produces the best results, meaning that there are no runs, no possibility of brush marks and almost no dust nibs. But the build is very slow, so it takes more coats than the other two methods to get the same look and protection against moisture.

FIRST COAT: The first coat soaks into the wood and seals it when the finish dries. So, even though you intend to wipe off the excess, you should apply a wet coat to all areas and keep it wet for several minutes. Add more finish to areas that become dull due to the finish soaking in. You can use this wipe-off method of applying wiping varnish to "shine up" other finishes that have become dull (be sure the surface is clean) or to make a brushed varnish or polyurethane almost perfect after you have sanded out the brush marks.

**1** If you choose to brush the finish, the fast, efficient method on flat, horizontal surfaces is to deposit a brush load of the wiping varnish onto the near edge and then spread it. Here, I'm using an inexpensive, throwaway bristle brush, called a "chip" brush, because I'm not worried about bristles falling out. They will be removed when I wipe off the excess finish.

**2** With a puddle of wiping varnish deposited, spread it end to end.

**3** You can use an inexpensive, throwaway, foam brush instead of a bristle brush.

**4** The most efficient way to apply wiping varnish when you intend to wipe off all the excess is simply to wipe it on. Wet your rag well with the finish, or pour some finish onto the wood and spread it around with the rag. You want to put on a wet coat so the wiping varnish penetrates well.

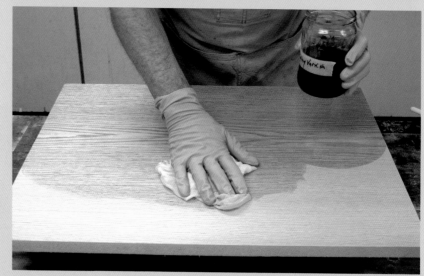

**5** With the surface well wetted, wipe off all the excess with a dry cloth. (You could also use a durable paper towel.) There's no need to scrub the surface. A little dampness won't hurt anything.

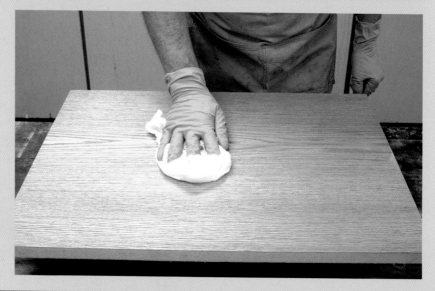

SAND SMOOTH: The surface always feels rough after the first coat. A critical step for achieving a smooth final result is to sand this coat smooth after it dries.

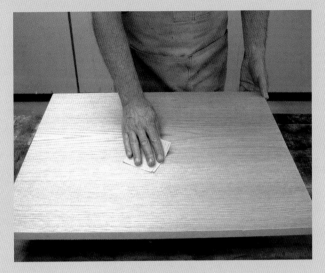

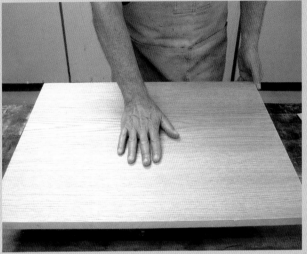

**6** After drying, sand the surface lightly using #320- or #400-grit sandpaper until the finish feels smooth. It shouldn't take much, usually not more than one or two passes everywhere. There's no reason to use a flat block to back the sandpaper. Abrading with sandpaper produces much better results than with steel wool or abrasive pads because sandpaper cuts off while the others merely round over.

**7** After removing the dust with a vacuum, tack rag or dust brush, wipe over the surface with your hand. You'll feel if there is any remaining dust and, as long as it's not much, you'll remove it with your hand. You can clean off your hand by wiping it on your pants leg.

MORE COATS: Keep applying coats (with six hours to overnight between each) until you're happy with the look of the finish. The procedure for each additional coat is the same. First, you sand and clean the surface as just described. Then you apply and wipe off the wiping varnish.

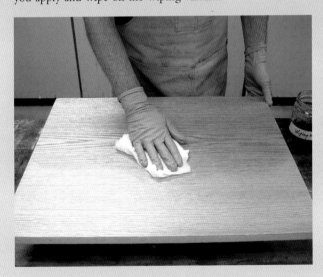

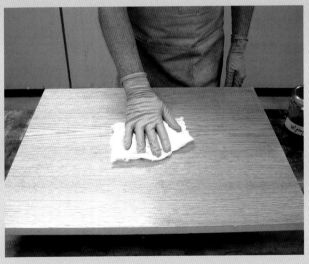

**8** Wipe a damp-to-wet coat of wiping varnish over the entire surface you're finishing. You don't need to make these coats as wet as the first because the finish can no longer soak into the wood.

**9** Wipe off the excess finish. You can leave the surface a little damp.

## DRY BRUSH EXCESS METHOD

Brush wet coats of wiping varnish onto the wood and remove some of the finish with a dry brush. This method leaves more build than wiping off the excess but still eliminates the possibility of runs and sags.

FIRST COAT: Brush a wet coat of wiping varnish over the surface as in the wiping–off method. You could also wipe on a wet coat with a cloth.

**1** (ABOVE RIGHT) With the surface wet with wiping varnish, dry your brush on a clean cloth.

**2** (RIGHT) Then brush back over to pick up some of the finish. At the beginning, dry the brush after each pass so you pick up the maximum amount of finish. If you decide to go over the surface a second time, you can make several passes before wiping. It's best to use a better-quality bristle brush that won't shed bristles.

**3** Watch what's happening in a reflected light. Your goal is to get an even thickness of finish without puddles on horizontal surfaces or runs on vertical surfaces.

**SAND SMOOTH:** It's always critical to sand after the first coat so the roughness doesn't telegraph through each additional coat.

**4** Sand the surface with #320- or #400-grit sandpaper. You can use just your hand to back the sandpaper. Make two or three passes everywhere until the finish feels smooth.

**5** There should be very little dust. You may be able to remove it with just your hand, wiping it on your pants leg. But you can use a vacuum, dust brush or a tack rag, then wipe with your hand to check that all the dust has been removed.

**MORE COATS:** All additional coats go on the same as the first. Apply as many as you need to get the look you want, allowing overnight drying for each in a warm room. Be sure to sand each coat smooth before applying another.

**6** Brush a wet coat of wiping varnish onto the surface. You don't have to be too careful how you brush because the dry brushing will smooth things out.

**7** With the entire surface wet, begin lifting some of the wiping varnish by brushing over with a dry brush.

**8** After each pass, dry your brush on a clean cloth. If you decide to dry brush the surface a second time, you can make more than one pass before drying the brush. You'll get the feel very quickly.

**9** The dry brushing method is perfect for vertical surfaces. You can also wipe off all the excess, of course, but dry brushing leaves a thicker build with each coat without runs or sags. Always watch what is happening in a reflected light — overhead, window or light on a stand — and dry brush to remove any problems you find.

## LEAVE EXCESS METHOD

Brush wet coats of wiping varnish onto the wood and leave them, allowing overnight drying between each. This can be done only on flat horizontal surfaces such as tabletops because of runs and sags. You can always use the dry-brushing technique to remove excess on edges and other connected vertical surfaces to avoid runs.

FIRST COAT: This is a brush on and leave method of applying wiping varnish. So it's just like brushing full strength varnish or polyurethane, or brushing paint.

**1** Deposit a brush load of wiping varnish onto the near edge of the panel. A brush load is the bristles dipped about one-third to one-half way into the wiping varnish, lifted out and plopped down on the wood.

**2** Stretch the wiping varnish out edge-to-edge. You don't have to be as careful with wiping varnish as you do with full strength varnish or polyurethane because wiping varnish levels well. You could even brush across the grain and the finish would still level so you don't see the brush marks.

**3** Continue depositing the wiping varnish and stretching it out across the surface.

**4** So as not to drag the bristles over the edge and cause runs down the side, use airplane-like landings about in inch or so in from each edge and brush across and off the other side.

**SAND SMOOTH:** The first coat of finish always causes a rough surface. You need to sand this smooth before continuing to the next coat.

**5** After drying, sand the surface lightly using #320- or #400-grit sandpaper until the finish feels smooth. It shouldn't take much, usually not more than one or two passes everywhere. There's no reason to use a flat block to back the sandpaper. Abrading with sandpaper produces much better results than with steel wool or abrasive pads because sandpaper cuts off while the others merely round over.

**6** Remove the sanding dust with a tack rag, vacuum or dust brush. A tack rag (shown here) or vacuum is best because brushing kicks dust into the air; the dust can then settle back onto a freshly applied finish and stick to it.

**7** Just before applying the next coat, wipe over the surface with your hand. You'll feel if there is any remaining dust and, as long as it's not much, you'll remove it with your hand. You can clean off your hand by wiping it on your pants leg.

**MORE COATS:** Brushing and leaving builds the finish much quicker than wiping off or dry brushing. But dust nibs are more likely because the finish remains tacky longer. Be sure to sand lightly between each coat. You're finished when you achieve the look you want.

8 Deposit a brush load of wiping varnish onto the near edge of the wood and stretch it out end-to-end.

9 Continue depositing brush loads and stretching them out across the surface.

**FINISH UP:** There are always some dust nibs stuck in the last coat of finish. As long as they are small and there aren't too many of them, you can remove them by rubbing with a brown paper bag.

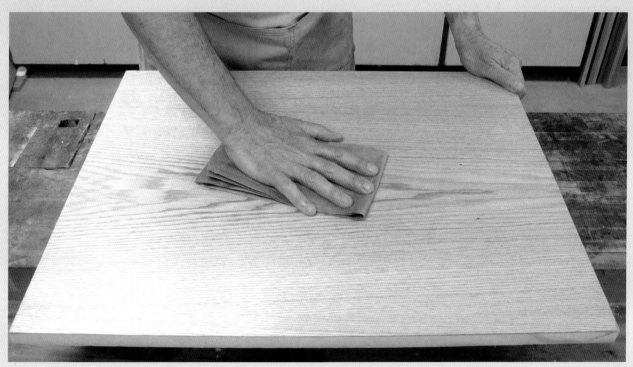

A brown paper bag works exceptionally well at removing the roughness caused by fine dust nibs stuck to the last coat. Simply fold the bag and rub the surface. To avoid scratches, it's best to allow the finish to dry to the point that you don't smell anything when you put your nose against the surface and take a whiff.

# Oil/Varnish Blend

Oil finishes have a very long history. There are countless references in early American and English writings mentioning the use of linseed oil for protecting objects ranging from the exterior of buildings to furniture to gunstocks.

Linseed oil is pressed from the seeds of the flax plant. Modern linseed oil is available in two forms: raw and "boiled." Raw linseed oil takes weeks to dry, even when all the excess is wiped off the wood. So there are no situations in interior woodworking where it would be advantageous to use raw linseed oil. Boiled linseed oil has liquid driers added that make the oil dry overnight in a warm room when the excess oil is wiped off. The oil is no longer boiled, but the traditional name is retained.

Lead was once used as a drier, but it is no longer. As with all finishes once they have dried, boiled linseed oil is safe to use on objects that will come in contact with food or mouths.

Tung oil, which is pressed from the nuts of the Chinese tung tree, became available in the West around 1900. This oil is more water resistant than linseed oil, so it is used in the manufacture of exterior spar varnishes. Tung oil is rarely used by itself as a wood finish, however, because it takes many coats to produce a nice result and each coat takes two or three days to dry when all the excess is wiped off. (See Chapter on Wiping Varnish to understand that many brands labeled "tung oil" are actually varnish thinned with paint thinner.)

Boiled linseed oil and tung oil can be mixed with varnish (including polyurethane varnish) in any proportion to make a finish that is just as easy to apply as boiled linseed oil but is a little more water resistant and dries quicker because of the

Linseed oil is sold in raw and "boiled" form. Raw linseed oil takes much too long to dry to be useful as an interior wood finish. Boiled linseed oil, which isn't actually boiled, dries overnight in a warm room when all the excess is wiped off the wood. You should always use boiled linseed oil, not raw linseed oil.

Tung oil is always sold as "100% tung oil" so far as I know. Just like both types of linseed oil, tung oil is also sold without thinners. So if a solvent is listed on the container, the product is not tung oil.

A number of manufacturers produce mixtures of linseed oil and varnish. The more common name used for this mixture is "Danish Oil." But as you can see from this picture, manufacturers are very creative in their naming.

varnish. Oil/varnish blends produce a soft satin sheen and are very popular with woodworkers.

For this exercise/project you will make your own mixture of oil and var-

nish using boiled linseed oil, polyurethane varnish and mineral spirits. The method of application is exactly the same as that for boiled linseed oil alone, so you could use it instead.

# Oil/Varnish Blend;
# Difficulty: Low.

## WHAT IS IT?

⅓ boiled linseed oil, ⅓ oil-based, gloss or satin polyurethane varnish, ⅓ mineral spirits (paint thinner).

## RULES FOR APPLICATION

• The first coat should be applied wet and left wet on the surface for 5-to-10 minutes, then wiped off.

• The excess of each coat has to be totally wiped off or the finish will dry sticky.

• Each coat requires overnight drying in a warm room, garage or shop.

• Two coats are necessary for good results. Three coats are usually better.

## WHEN TO USE

Limited to objects not subject to excessive abuse or contact with water because the finish dries too soft to resist scratches and too thin to resist water penetration. Examples include: shelves, trim, beds, some chests-of-drawers, curio cabinets, chairs and some entertainment centers.

## COMPATIBILITY

Can be used under any finish (or paint) as long as the oil/varnish blend has fully dried (at least a week in a warm room). Oil/varnish blend can also be used over any stain, over older oil finishes, or to add shine over any finish that has dulled or been worn. Be sure to wipe off all the excess.

## ADVANTAGES

• The easiest, most foolproof finish to apply: simply wipe on and wipe off.

• Produces a soft satin sheen and a very thin "close-to-the-wood" appearance.

• Adds depth and richness to dark and dark-stained woods.

Here's how to tell if a commercial product is an oil/varnish blend. The label doesn't say "raw linseed oil," "boiled linseed oil" or "100% tung oil, and a puddle of the finish dries to a soft wrinkled state after several days. In fact, it remains soft enough to puncture with your fingernail for months or years.

## DISADVANTAGES

• Weak resistance to abuse and water.

• Adds a noticeable yellow/orange coloring to light-colored woods.

• Can spontaneously combust if rags are piled on top of each other.

## COMMON APPLICATION PROBLEMS

• Sticky result when all the excess finish isn't wiped off.

• "Bleeding" of the finish from the wood's pores.

## MAKE YOUR OWN

• One part boiled linseed oil; one part gloss or satin polyurethane varnish; one part mineral spirits.

## VARIATIONS

• Add less or no mineral spirits.

• Substitute 100% tung oil for boiled linseed oil.

• Substitute ½ part boiled linseed oil and ½ part 100% tung oil for one part boiled linseed oil.

• Substitute any oil-based varnish for polyurethane varnish.

• Add more oil and less varnish for a longer working time (rarely necessary).

• Add more varnish and less oil for slightly more water resistance and gloss.

## WHAT YOU NEED

- A 16"-by-24" or larger panel of ½" or ¾" veneered plywood or MDF. Any hardwood veneer is OK. (From your scraps, a wood supplier or from one of many cabinet shops that often throw away pieces this size.)

(The following items are all available from a home center, paint store or woodworking store or catalog/website.)

- A pint or quart of boiled linseed oil.
- A pint or quart of oil-based, gloss or satin polyurethane.
- A pint or quart of mineral spirits (paint thinner).
- A clean wide-mouth plastic container, jar or coffee can with a lid. (Also from your kitchen.)
- Latex or other protective gloves.
- Lint-free rags such as old, clean T-

shirts, cheesecloth or durable paper "rags," which are soft paper towels in a box or roll sold to painters. (Also from your old clothes.)

- A sheet of #400- or #600-grit sandpaper.
- A tack rag (optional).

## MAKING OIL/VARNISH BLEND

You have more control over the application and performance characteristics of an oil/varnish blend if you make your own. Begin with the basic formula here, then make adjustments to your satisfaction.

**1** To make your own oil/varnish blend for this exercise/project, pour approximately equal parts of boiled linseed oil, oil-based polyurethane varnish and mineral spirits into a wide-mouth jar, coffee can or plastic container. Be sure to use oil-based polyurethane (cleans up with mineral spirits), not water-based polyurethane (cleans up with water). You can use either gloss or satin polyurethane varnish. It won't make much difference. It's the oil part that produces the soft satin sheen.

**2** The three parts remain separated after you have poured them together. You won't notice this if you are pouring into a can.

**3** Stir the mixture of oil, polyurethane and thinner so they combine. You won't need to stir again.

FIRST COAT: You can reduce the number of coats necessary by keeping the first coat wet on the wood for five or ten minutes to allow the finish to soak in well.

**4** Pour some of the oil/varnish blend onto a horizontal panel. You can brush the finish instead, but doing this is much slower. You can also pour some of the finish onto a cloth and wipe it wet onto the wood.

**5** Spread the finish all over the panel with a cloth. Wear gloves, of course.

**6** Keep the surface wet for five minutes or so and look in a reflected light for any areas that become dull because the oil has soaked in.

**7** Rewet all the dull areas as many times as necessary until they remain wet. The purpose of this is to fully seal less dense areas so that fewer subsequent coats will be necessary to get an even sheen across the surface.

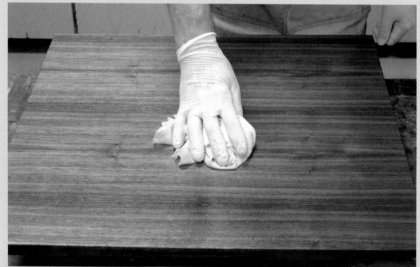

**8** When all areas remain wet on the surface for several minutes, you can move to the next step.

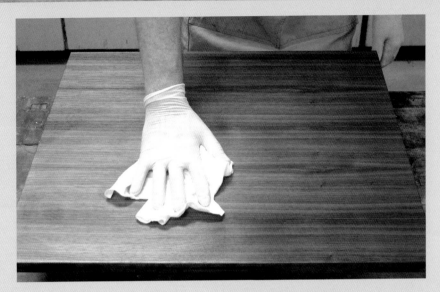

**9** Wipe off all the excess oil/varnish blend with a dry cloth. Emphasis on ALL. Don't leave any dampness or the surface will remain sticky for a long time..

**10** On large-pored woods such as this oak, some oil/varnish blend may bleed back out of the pores, creating shiny puddles over the heavy grain. This happens more when the temperature is high and rarely after the first coat. You should wipe off this bleeding until it stops, usually within several hours. Check the surface every 30 minutes of so. If the bleeding dries hard, rub the surface with #0000 steel wool to dull the gloss, then apply another coat. If the problem is so bad that you can't fix it with steel wool, strip the finish with paint stripper and begin again.

**MORE COATS:** You don't get a nice sheen with any finish after just the first coat. You have to let it dry, then sand it smooth and apply at least one more coat of finish to get a finished look.

---

**11** After drying overnight the surface will feel a little rough. The first coat of every finish causes this, and the goal is always to end up with a finish that feels smooth.

**12** When the surface is dry to the touch, sand it lightly using #320- or #400-grit sandpaper to make it feel smooth. It shouldn't take much, usually not more than one or two passes everywhere. Always sand in the direction of the wood grain and use your hand to back the sandpaper. There's nothing gained by using a flat block to back the sandpaper because you aren't sanding enough to dig hollows into the wood. You could also use #0000 steel wool or an abrasive pad to smooth the surface, but these don't cut off the nibs as well as sandpaper does. Steel wool and abrasive pads round over rather than cut off. If the oil/varnish blend gums up on the sandpaper when you're sanding between coats, the finish hasn't dried enough. The room may be too cold or you may not have removed all the excess. If the first, remove the excess by wiping with a strong solvent such as naphtha or lacquer thinner and apply another coat. If the second, let the finish dry longer in a warmer room.

**13** After dusting the surface, pour some more of the oil/varnish blend onto the surface. You don't have to be concerned about dust on the surface or in the air when finishing with an oil/varnish blend because you wipe off all the excess after each coat. You will remove any dust that has been left or that has settled.

**14** Just as with the first coat, spread the puddle all over the surface. You can brush the finish if you want, but it is considerably slower. Or you can wet a cloth and wipe on a wet coat. With the second and subsequent coats, nothing is gained by letting the oil/varnish blend remain wet on the surface for several minutes. You can wipe off all the excess without waiting. Continue applying coats once each day until you aren't seeing any improvement. It's rarely necessary to apply more than three coats.

ULTIMATE FINISH: Because you're wiping off all the excess with an oil finish, you can sand the wood while it's wet with finish. You'll wipe off all the sludge you create, and the finish lubricates the sandpaper so it scratches less.

To get a result that feels a little smoother and has a slightly "softer" satin sheen, sand each coat after the first with #600-grit (black) sandpaper while the wood is still wet with the finish. Sand in the direction of the wood grain using your hand to back the sandpaper. Several passes over all areas are sufficient. Then wipe off all the excess finish. You can do this with each coat after the first. You won't gain anything by sanding the first coat wet because sanding just the second coat will bring you to the same smoothness. With this method, there's no benefit to sanding between coats, so skip that step. You get slightly better results because the finish acts as a lubricant for the sandpaper. Be careful using this method, however, if you have stained the wood under the finish. You may remove some of the stain and leave some areas lighter.

**VERTICAL AND COMPLEX SURFACES:** Oil finishes are very easy to apply to vertical and three-dimensional surfaces. Simply wipe on, keep wet for a few minutes, and wipe off.

**1** **(ABOVE LEFT)** To apply an oil/varnish blend to vertical and complex surfaces, wet a cloth with the finish and wipe it onto the wood, making the wood wet (just short of dripping) for the first coat. Follow the same procedure of keeping duller areas wet until they remain damp.

**2** **(ABOVE RIGHT)** When you are satisfied that the first coat of oil/varnish blend has soaked the wood enough, wipe off all the excess with a dry cloth. For subsequent coats, simply wiping with a wet cloth is sufficient. There's no need to leave the surface wet for five minutes.

**3** **(RIGHT)** Pay special attention to getting all the oil/varnish blend wiped from inside corners, grooves and other recesses. Otherwise, these areas will remain sticky for a very long time.

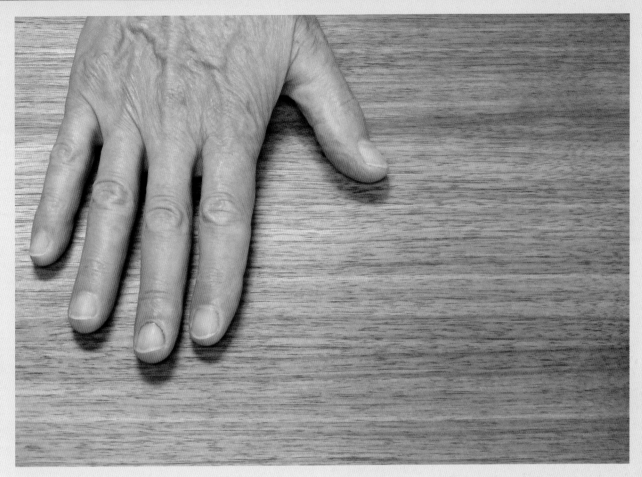

FINISHED: Knowing when to stop is always a question, especially with oil/varnish blends because the look and feel changes so little after the second coat. When you are happy with the look and feel of the finished wood, you're done. This happens sometimes after the second coat, usually after the third. But you can apply as many coats as you want as long as you are seeing some improvement.

## Oily Rags

Oily rags may be the most dangerous item you have in your shop because they can spontaneously combust if left in a pile or thrown wet into a trashcan. Caution! It's very important that you hang your oily rags to dry right after you finish. Oily rags can spontaneously combust and burn down your shop or house if not spread out so air can get to all sides. Never throw wet oily rags into a trashcan or pile them on top of each other. If you are working with others, have everyone immerse their rags in a pail of water, then take them out at the end of the day and hang them individually to dry. Once dry (and hardened) the rags are safe to throw in the trash. They are no different than wood with a dried oil finish.

# Polyurethane

Oil-based polyurethane is a type of varnish. In common speech it's usually referred to simply as "polyurethane."

The polyurethane part of the varnish makes the finish more water, scratch, heat and solvent resistant than other types of varnish, but common alkyd varnish is still more resistant than all other finishes discussed in this book, including water-based polyurethane. You won't notice any difference in the ap-plication characteristics of polyurethane varnish and other types of oil-based varnish, so you could substitute any of these for the polyurethane used in this exercise/project.

Just as with all varnishes, polyure-thane is the easiest finish to apply using a brush because it dries slowly enough to give you plenty of time to brush it out, even onto large and complex sur-faces. But the slow drying also leads to problems — specifically dust settling and getting stuck in the finish and a greater likelihood of runs and sags.

Polyurethane is the finish you should use if you want the best protec-tion (against moisture) and durability (scratch, heat and solvent resistance).

For this exercise/project you can use any brand of polyurethane, or you can substitute any type of varnish if you'd like. They all apply the same.

There are several common types of varnish. From the left, below: spar varnish that is more elastic for use outdoors, common indoor, alkyd varnish, boat varnish with UV-light absorbers added for better protection against sunlight, polyurethane varnish with a name that could be misleading if you don't use some imagination, and common polyurethane varnish.

# Oil-Based Polyurethane; Difficulty: Low.

## WHAT IS IT?

Polyurethane is the most popular type of varnish. It's made with alkyd and polyurethane resins cooked with oil, usually modified soybean (soya) oil. A more technical name is "uralkyd."

## VARIATIONS

Polyurethane varies in sheen (amount of gloss) depending on how much "flatting agent" is added. Common sheens are gloss, semi-gloss, satin, matte and flat. The sheen will be listed on the label, but there is no consistency among manufacturers about the meaning of each term.

## THINS AND CLEANS UP WITH

Mineral spirits (paint thinner).

## HOW TO IDENTIFY

All brands of oil-based polyurethane are labeled "polyurethane" or something similar such as Defthane, Varathane or Kel-thane. Labeling often doesn't make so clear the distinction between oil-based polyurethane and water-based polyurethane, however. You can tell which is which by looking at the thinning and clean-up solvent listed on the container. Mineral spirits (sometimes referred to as "petroleum distillate" or "aliphatic hydrocarbon") indicate oil-based polyurethane. Water indicates water-based polyurethane.

## RULES FOR APPLICATION

- Brush back and forth in the direction of the wood grain, stretching the finish from end to end — just like painting.
- Watch what's happening in a reflected light, especially when brushing vertical surfaces, so you can see runs and sags as they develop and brush them out.
- Try to work in temperatures ranging between 65°F and 80°F for easiest application and best results.
- Allow to cure thoroughly before sanding or applying another coat. Overnight in a warm room is usually adequate. The finish should be dry enough so it powders when sanded.

## WHEN TO USE

Whenever you want excellent protection (against moisture) and durability (scratch, heat and solvent resistance). Examples would be floors, kitchen and bathroom cabinets and tabletops, though you can use polyurethane on any wood object. Oil-based polyurethane is the most protective and durable of all typically brushed finishes.

## COMPATIBILITY

You can apply polyurethane over any stain or finish as long as it is dry, clean and dull. The best way to achieve dullness is to sand or steel wool the surface. You can also apply any finish over polyurethane as long as it is dry, clean and dull. But apply a barrier coat of shellac before using lacquer because the strong lacquer-thinner solvent could cause blistering.

## ADVANTAGES

- Easy brush application.
- The most protective (against moisture) and durable (scratch, heat and solvent resistant) of all common finishes.
- Available in infinite sheens from high-gloss to flat.

## DISADVANTAGES

- Long drying time makes it susceptible to dust nibs and runs.
- Can take on a plastic appearance after many coats.
- Adds a yellow/orange tone to light-colored woods.

## COMMON APPLICATION PROBLEMS

- A rough surface caused by not sanding the first coat smooth or by dust nibs.
- Runs and sags.
- Bubbles in the finish.
- Brush marks.
- Doesn't dry well because of low temperatures or oily resin in the wood.

## WHAT YOU NEED

- A 16"-by-24" or larger sheet of ½" or ¾" veneered plywood or MDF. Any hardwood veneer is OK. (From your scraps, a wood supplier or one of many cabinet shops that often throw away pieces this size.)
- A pint or quart of oil-based poly-urethane — gloss or satin. (From a home center, paint store or wood-working store or catalogue.)
- A quart of mineral spirits. (From a home center, paint store or wood-working store or catalogue.)
- A tall jar with a wide enough open-ing for the paintbrush to go through. (From your kitchen.)
- A two-inch-wide paintbrush. Any brush will do, including natural bris-tle, synthetic bristle or foam. (From a home center, paint store or wood-working store or catalogue.)

- A sheet of #320- or #400-grit sandpaper. (From a home center, paint store or woodworking store or catalogue.)

- A shop vacuum, compressed air, dust brush or tack rag. (Tack rag from a home center, paint store or wood-working store or catalogue.)
- Paint strainers.

## PREPARE THE POLYURETHANE

Gloss polyurethane is ready to go because there's nothing to stir into suspension. All other sheens of the finish have to be stirred. It's always a good idea work out of a container sepa-rate from your source to keep it clean.

**1** Stir the polyurethane to the bottom of the can if you are using anything but gloss. It's not necessary (but doesn't hurt anything) to stir gloss.

**2** Pour approximately enough polyurethane for the job at hand into a clean jar or can with an opening larger than the width of your brush. Working out of a separate container ensures that your main supply stays clean. It's always best to pour through a paint strainer to remove small particles of dust or dirt.

**FIRST COAT:** If you are staining the wood, do so before applying the first coat of polyurethane. The first coat will raise the wood grain a little, so this coat should be sanded smooth after it dries.

---

**1** Before starting to brush, use your hand to wipe over the entire surface to be sure the wood is clean. If dirty, vacuum (best) or blow or brush off the dust with compressed air or a dust brush. Blowing or brushing kicks dust into the air, and it will settle back on your newly applied finish. So you should do this in another location, then bring the panel back to the finishing area. Wipe over again with your hand and wipe off any dust you pick up onto your pants leg.

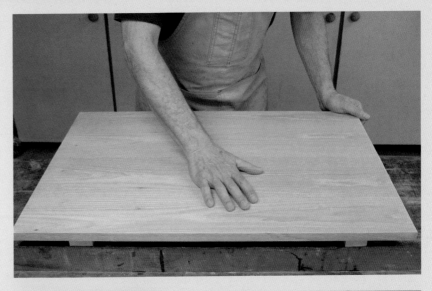

**2** Always brush the most important surfaces last. In this case the edges are less important than the top, so I'm brushing the edges first.

**3** On large horizontal surfaces the efficient way to apply a finish with a brush is to lift a brush load of finish out of the container and deposit it onto the surface. A brush load is finish about halfway up the bristles, not all the way up to the metal. There's no point in tapping the brush against the side of the container or dragging the brush over the lip of the container unless you want to remove some of the finish so it doesn't drip. If you hold the container near where you intend to deposit the finish, dripping won't matter because you'll brush it out, and you will get the maximum amount of finish transferred. You could even pour some finish onto the surface and spread it with your brush.

**4** (ABOVE LEFT) With some finish deposited in the middle of the area you intend to brush, spread or "stretch" the finish end-to-end by brushing back and fourth. If there isn't enough finish to create wetness end-to-end, deposit more.

**5** (ABOVE RIGHT) To keep from dragging your brush over the edge and creating runs, bring the brush down onto the surface in an airplane landing motion about an inch in from one edge and move the brush across the surface and off the other edge. Make two or three strokes back and forth this way to line up brush strokes and knock off bubbles that might have been introduced by the brushing.

**6** (LEFT) With the first brush load brushed end-to-end, deposit another brush load within an inch or so of the first brush strokes.

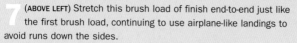

**7** (ABOVE LEFT) Stretch this brush load of finish end-to-end just like the first brush load, continuing to use airplane-like landings to avoid runs down the sides.

**8** (ABOVE RIGHT) With the second brush load brushed end-to-end, brush it back into the first brushed area so it all appears as one. It's important to get this second (and continuing) brush strokes laid down and brushed back into the previous strokes before they begin to set up. This is called "keeping a wet edge." If the already brushed area is beginning to set up, the brush will drag this finish and create severe brush marks, which you will have to sand out after the finish has dried.

**9** (RIGHT) Continue in the same manner across the surface until you have covered it all.

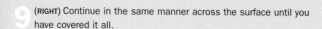

**10** As you move across the surface, watch what is happening in reflected light. It is only by doing this that you know you're doing everything properly. This is the one critical instruction that you rarely see. Notice the roughness the finish is causing in the wood. This is normal for the first coat, and you'll sand it out after it dries.

**11** If you want to use the same brush again within several days, you can avoid having to clean it if you wrap it tightly in plastic wrap so no air can get in, or scrunch the bristles against the bottom of a jar or can of mineral spirits, then hang it in the container with the mineral spirits covering at least a quarter way up the bristles. Notice the extra hole I drilled in the brush handle so the brush hangs with its bristles not touching the bottom of the jar. If the bristles rest on the bottom, they may become permanently bent.

SAND FIRST COAT: Possibly the most critical step for achieving good final results is to sand the first coat smooth before moving on to apply the second coat. The first coat of finish is always rough, and if you don't sand it smooth, the roughness will telegraph through all additional coats.

**12** After overnight drying in a warm room, the polyurethane should be totally dry to the touch. You need to sand out the roughness that is always created by the first coat of any finish. Use #320- or #400-grit sandpaper. Surely no coarser than #220 grit. There's no reason to back the sandpaper with a flat sanding block.

You are just removing the slight roughness created by the first coat and any dust that has settled. You won't be cutting into the wood. It shouldn't take more than three or four passes everywhere. There's no need to sand more than it takes to make the surface feel smooth to your hand.

**13** The finish should be dry enough so it powders when sanded.

**14** If the finish doesn't powder, it isn't dry enough. Most likely, the room is too cold and you should turn up the heat, or give the finish much longer to dry.

**MORE COATS:** You can apply as many coats as you want, but two or three are usually adequate. Three coats are best for floors, kitchen cabinets and tabletops that will receive a lot of wear and contact with moisture.

**15** If the sanding has created a lot of dust, remove it with a vacuum (best), dust brush or compressed air. Then wipe the surface with a tack rag. This is a widely available sticky cloth that picks up dust well. You could substitute a cloth lightly dampened with mineral spirits.

**16** Just before starting to brush, wipe with your hand to be sure the surface is clean.

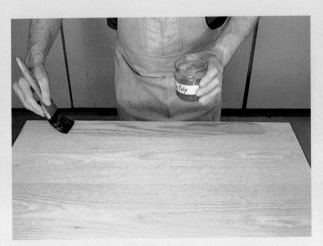

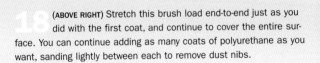

**17** (ABOVE LEFT) After brushing the edges, deposit a brush load of finish near the front edge just as you did with the first coat.

**18** (ABOVE RIGHT) Stretch this brush load end-to-end just as you did with the first coat, and continue to cover the entire surface. You can continue adding as many coats of polyurethane as you want, sanding lightly between each to remove dust nibs.

**19** (RIGHT) You will always have some dust nibs in your final coat of finish. If they are small and few, you can usually remove them by rubbing the surface with a folded brown paper bag after the finish has hardened completely — that is, there is no smell when you put your nose against the finish and take a whiff.

BRUSH BOTH SIDES: If you'd like to brush both sides of a tabletop or cabinet door in one session, you can use a "nail" board to make this possible. Nail boards are easy to make.

**1** You can brush both sides of flat panels and cabinet doors without having to wait for one side to dry by using a nail board like the one pictured here — except I used drywall screws instead of nails. These screws have very tiny pointed tips that make virtually unnoticeable pricks in the finish and wood.

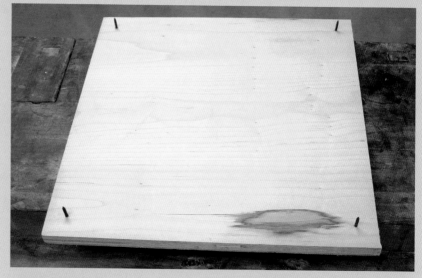

**2** Begin by brushing the backside or underside, and don't brush the edges.

**3** With the backside complete, turn the panel or cabinet door over and lay it on the nails (screws) with the just completed side facing down.

**4** Then brush the front or topside including the edges. If some drips form on the bottom of the edges, wipe them off with a cloth.

**5** You can use an inexpensive throwaway foam brush instead of a bristle brush. However, foam brushes are more difficult to use effectively on complex surfaces.

**6** You can also use an inexpensive throwaway "chip" brush instead of a more expensive bristle brush. The difference is that the chip brush sheds more bristles and doesn't hold as much finish.

## Brushing Vertical

Brushing vertical surfaces is more difficult than brushing horizontal surfaces because of the greater likelihood of runs and sags. Watch for them developing by looking into a reflected light from overhead, a window or a light on a stand, and brush them out. Brush vertical surfaces the same as horizontal surfaces in the sense of brushing end-to-end with the grain and keeping a wet edge. To avoid dripping you usually have to remove some of the excess finish from the brush by tapping the bristles against the side of the container or dragging them over the lip. It's critical that you watch the area you're brushing in a reflected light so you can see any runs or sags as they develop. Then simply brush them out and deposit the excess finish your brush picks up on a non-brushed area or back in the container.

## Brush Complex Surfaces

When brushing complex surfaces, always brush the least important surfaces first and the most important surfaces last. This procedure increases the chances that the most important surfaces come out free of flaws. On this mass-produced, unfinished child's chair, I'm brushing the legs and stretchers before turning the chair upright and brushing the back and seat. Often, it's easier to brush perpendicular to the grain on turnings — that is, around the turning rather than lengthways.

# Common Problems

It's not possible to brush polyurethane without any problems. This is mostly due to the slow drying of the finish.

I've already shown you how to deal with dust nibs and brush marks. Here are some additional problems.

**1** If you catch runs or sags in a reflected light while the polyurethane is still wet, brush them out. If they dry on you, you'll have to sand or scrape them off before applying another coat. You can use a razor blade to scrape off the build. It's easiest (but not always convenient) to remove a run or sag after it has hardened all the way through, which could take several days.

**2** Bubbles, which are caused much more by the turbulence created by brushing than by stirring or shaking the can, usually pop out on their own — except in hot temperatures when the polyurethane may skin over too quickly. Help the popping-out along by brushing back over after each brush stroke. If bubbles dry in the finish, you'll have to sand them out and apply another coat. Thin this coat with 10% to 30% mineral spirits to give the bubbles more time to pop out on their own. This coat will be thinner on the surface, so you may have to apply more coats to get the thickness you want.

**3** The most common reason a finish doesn't dry well is that the temperature is too low. Warm the room by turning up the heat or place a heat lamp on the areas that are still sticky. A second reason for slow drying with polyurethane is that the wood contains a natural oily resin that interferes with the drying. The woods that contain this resin feel oily to the touch and grow in jungles. Examples are teak, rosewood and cocobolo. Heat will promote drying, but the ultimate cure is to remove the oily resin from the surface by wiping with naphtha before you apply the finish. Apply the finish just after the naphtha evaporates from the surface. You can also apply a first coat of shellac to seal off the oily resin before applying the polyurethane. If you have already applied the finish before discovering that it won't dry, try turning up the heat. If this doesn't work, you'll have to strip the finish and start over, first wiping the wood with naphtha. Once the first coat has dried and locked in the oily resin, additional coats will dry fine, as long as the temperature isn't too low—above 70° being best.

**4** If there's enough air left in a can or jar of polyurethane that has had some of its finish removed, the polyurethane will skin over (as shown in this picture). If you remove the skin and the polyurethane is still liquid underneath, it is fine to use. Strain the finish to be sure no parts of the skin remain. The easy way to avoid the skinning is to transfer the remainder of a can of polyurethane to a smaller container so there's no air to cause the skinning. The best container is probably a jar with a lid that fits tight. Label the jar.

## BRUSH MARKS

You can't avoid brush marks brushing full strength polyurethane. The trick to getting it brush-mark free is to sand the last coat level, then apply a coat or two of thinned polyurethane. Thinned finishes level better than thick finishes.

**1** If you want to eliminate brush marks at any step along the way or after your final coat, sand them out. Be sure to back your sandpaper with a flat block so you sand off the ridges rather than round them over. Use a grit sandpaper that cuts through the problem efficiently without creating larger than necessary scratches that then have to be sanded out — most likely, 220-, 280- or 320-grit sandpaper. If on the coarser side, sand again with a finer grit sandpaper to remove the coarser scratches so they don't show through the next coat of finish.

**2** To improve efficiency, especially on large surfaces, use a lubricant and wet/dry (black) sandpaper. This will keep the sandpaper from loading up with lumps of finish. The most effective lubricants are mineral oil and mineral spirits (odorless for less smell). The problem with using a lubricant is that you can't see what's happening, so remove it often to check, or scrape it off sections using a plastic spreader.

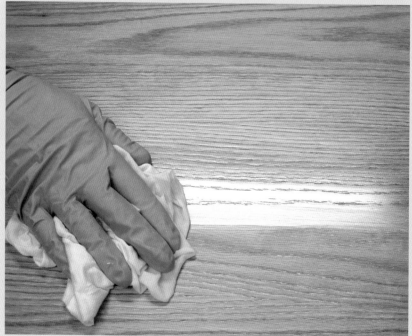

**3** Here the brush marks are sanded out. The shiny places are depressions in the grain, which I have left.

**4** Now to get a near perfect finish, thin the polyurethane a quarter-to-a-half with mineral spirits and wipe or brush it on. Then wipe or dry brush it off the surface, as described in the chapter on Wiping Varnish. You may need to apply several coats to fill in the sanding scratches.

## TIP: Washing Off a Coat of Polyurethane

If you notice problems, such as excessive dirt in the finish, you can wash off a coat of polyurethane with a mineral-spirits soaked cloth for about 30 minutes without damaging the coat underneath. Then brush on another coat after correcting the situation that caused the problem.

# Oil Stains and Polyurethane

Stains are used to change the color of wood and also make it look richer and deeper. There are three broad categories of stains that are widely available to amateurs: oil-based stains, water-based stains and gel stains. This chapter is about oil-based stains (also called "oil stains").

Oil stains are the easiest of all stains to use because they dry slowly so you have plenty of time to get them onto the wood and get the excess wiped off. These stains produce excellent results under any finish except water-based finishes (those that thin and clean up with water). With these finishes, you should let the oil stain dry for several days or longer in a warm room so the water-based finish can flow out and bond well. Or use a water-based stain instead.

## Oil Stains & Polyurethane; Difficulty: Low.

### WHAT IS IT?

Oil stain is a colorant (pigment or dye) added to some linseed oil and thinned with a lot of mineral spirits. Oil stains are often called "wiping" stains and sometimes "pigment" stains, though all stains can be wiped and most contain pigment.

### VARIATIONS

Oil stains differ in the ratio of colorant to binder and thinner, and also in whether pigment, dye or both are used as the colorant. The ratio of colorant to binder and thinner affects how dark the stain colors the wood.

### THINS AND CLEANS UP WITH

Mineral spirits (paint thinner).

### HOW TO IDENTIFY

Any liquid stain that thins and cleans up with mineral spirits. Manufacturers seldom list mineral spirits as an ingredient, however. They usually list "petroleum distillate" or "aliphatic hydrocarbon," which describes the same thing.

### RULES FOR APPLICATION

- Wipe, brush or spray a wet coat onto the wood.
- Wipe off the excess before the stain dries.

## WHEN TO USE

On any wood to change its color (darker, not lighter) and add definition (depth) to the grain.

## COMPATIBILITY

You can apply any finish over oil stain as long as the stain is dry. You can also apply an oil stain over any finish (for example, to color in some dings and scratches), but you should then apply another coat of finish to keep the colorant from being rubbed off. All stains that thin with mineral spirits can be mixed to adjust the color.

## ADVANTAGES

- To change the color of the wood.
- To make a cheaper or plainer wood look like a more expensive wood.
- To give yourself significantly more working time (to get the stain applied and wiped off) than you have with a water-based stain or dye stain.
- When the excess is wiped off, oil stain accentuates the grain making it look deeper and usually richer.

## DISADVANTAGES

- Highlights flaws in wood, including mill marks (the tool marks left by the machines that mill the lumber), dents, gouges and scratches. You have to get these sanded out before applying the stain.
- Highlights "blotching" in woods such as pine and cherry.
- Makes end grain darker unless it is sanded well.

## COMMON APPLICATION PROBLEMS

- Highlighting of flaws.
- Making end grain too dark.

## MAKE YOUR OWN

You can make your own oil stain from concentrated linseed-oil or Japan colorants available at paint stores, art-supply stores and woodworking stores and catalogs/websites. Simply thin the colorant with mineral spirits to get the color intensity you want.

## WHAT YOU NEED

(The following items are all available from a home center, paint store or woodworking store or catalog/website.)

- A pint or quart of oil-based wiping stain.
- A pint or quart of oil-based polyurethane.
- A wide-mouth container.
- Mineral spirits.
- Protective gloves.
- Wood conditioner.
- Brushes.
- Stirring sticks.
- A paint strainer (optional).
- #320- or #400-grit sandpaper.
- A brown paper bag.
- A tack rag (optional).
- Lint-free rags or durable paper towels.

## PREPARE THE STAIN

Most stains contain pigment that has to be stirred into suspension before use. Stir to the bottom of the can to be sure you reach all the pigment.

**1** You can use a stirring stick to check for pigment by scraping along the bottom of a can that has sat undisturbed for a week or longer.

**2** Always stir the stain before each use. Pigment can lump hard enough to make hand shaking ineffective. Stir to the bottom of the can to be effective.

## APPLY STAIN

Stain can be applied with rags, brushes or spray guns. Brushes are slow. A spray gun requires serious cleaning if you plan to use it with any other coating. Consider using rags.

**3** The easy way to apply stain is to wipe it on the wood. You can wipe in any direction or in circles. You can speed the process on horizontal surfaces by pouring on the stain and spreading it with a cloth. For vertical surfaces get the cloth soaking wet and spread the stain. You can also brush the stain, of course, but it is much slower.

**4** Wipe off the excess stain with a clean, dry cloth. You can wipe in any direction or in circles as long as you remove all the excess. But it's good practice to make your last wiping strokes go in the direction of the wood grain so any streaks you might leave will be disguised by the grain. Let the stain dry overnight before applying more stain (to make the color darker) or a finish.

**5** (LEFT) Wiping is much faster than brushing, but you may find brushing helpful for getting the stain into inside corners, grooves and recesses. Inexpensive, throw-away brushes, called "chip" brushes, are very useful here because bristle shedding isn't a problem. You will remove the bristles when you wipe off the excess stain.

**6** (BELOW LEFT) Wiping rather than brushing is more important on large surfaces such as this stereo cabinet. It would be very difficult to get the stain brushed everywhere and wiped off before drying. I've never had a problem getting stain into inside corners using a soaking wet cloth.

**7** (BELOW RIGHT) Oil stain rags are a potential fire hazard because of spontaneous combustion. To be safe, drape used rags over the edge of a trashcan or table, or spread them on the floor so air can get to all sides. When the rags are dry, and usually somewhat hardened, it's safe to throw them in the trash.

## APPLY FINISH

When the oil stain has dried, usually after about a day, you can applying any finish. But you should let the stain dry for a week before applying a water-based finish. Always apply a finish over stain so it doesn't get rubbed off.

**1** Apply polyurethane as described in the polyurethane chapter, beginning by depositing a brush load of the finish.

**2** Then stretch the finish to the ends of the surface.

# Wood Conditioners

Wood conditioner, or stain controller, is a difficult material to use and seldom produces desirable results. I recommend you put off using it until you have had considerable finishing experience. Instead, use gel stain, which is very effective against blotching on pine and somewhat effective on tight-grained hardwoods, such as cherry, birch and maple.

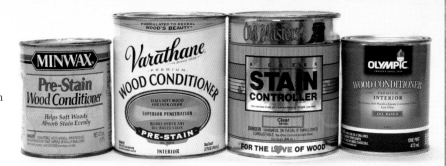

Most makers of varnishes also make wood conditioners and stain controllers. Here are four common brands.

**1** Wood conditioner is a simple product — varnish thinned with about two parts mineral spirits. It's also easy enough to apply. Simply brush on a wet coat and leave to dry.

**2** When the wood conditioner has dried, sand very lightly with #400-grit sandpaper — just enough to make the surface feel smooth.

**3** On this pine board, I applied wood conditioner to the left side, let it dry overnight, then sanded lightly with #400-grit sandpaper. Now I'm applying stain, and you can clearly see that the wood conditioner is blocking the penetration of the stain while the right side is becoming very blotched.

**4** The wood conditioner has prevented the blotching, but it has also reduced the coloring effect of the stain to almost nothing.

**5** **(LEFT)** With some experience and practice, you can learn the right amount of wood conditioner to apply to get the results you want, but you can't get both a dark coloring and no blotching. On this pine board, I reduced the amount of wood conditioner I applied and got a darker coloring, but I also started to bring out the blotching.

**6** **(BELOW)** Be aware that most manufacturers provide poor directions on the cans. Most say to apply the stain within two hours. On this board, I applied the stain directly to the wood on the left section. Then I applied wood conditioner to the rest of the board. I applied the same stain to the second section immediately, to the third after 10 minutes, to the fourth after two hours and to the right section of the board the next day after the thinned varnish had dried thoroughly. Notice that the blotching got increasingly worse until I let the wood conditioner fully dry. This is a difficult product to use effectively. I recommend you use gel stain, instead, when you want to reduce blotching.

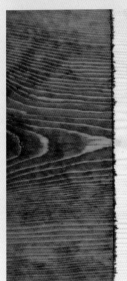

## End Grain

The grain at the ends of boards often colors much darker than the side grain. This is due, primarily, to it having not been sanded well enough. It's rougher, so more stain lodges in the recesses, which makes the wood darker. When end grain is cut, the wood tears, making it much rougher than the side grain. If you don't sand well enough, this end grain stains much darker. On this end grain, I sanded the left side smooth but left the right side as it came from the saw. Most people sand the end grain just like the side grain, but you need to sand much more to get an even color.

# Gel Stains and Polyurethane

Gel stains are a relatively new type of stain whose market is a little confused. These stains are widely available in home centers, and they solve one of the most discouraging problems in wood finishing — blotching. Blotching is uneven coloring in pine and some tight-grained hardwoods, such as cherry, birch and maple, caused by natural variations in the wood, not by how the stain is applied or by how well it is sanded and prepared.

The distinguishing characteristic of a gel stain is its thickness; it is thick like mayonnaise. Despite the thickness, gel stain spreads and wipes off easily, also like mayonnaise. The thickness and reduced flow of gel stain is what makes it effective at reducing blotching, which is caused by the uneven penetration of liquid stains. Gel stain doesn't penetrate much. It stays near the surface, creating a more even coloring.

This is great for woods that are blotch prone, especially pine. But it is not good for woods with a beautiful figure you want to highlight. In other words, gel stains are a specialty stain. They are good for some situations, but not for all.

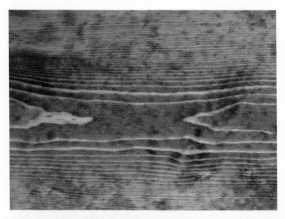

This is what blotching looks like in pine. Not all pine boards blotch, but most do. Often, the first wood a budding woodworker uses is pine. Then he or she typically stains the pine to make it look like walnut, cherry, mahogany or some other darker wood. The result is an ugly blotching that leads to that woodworker hating finishing ever after.

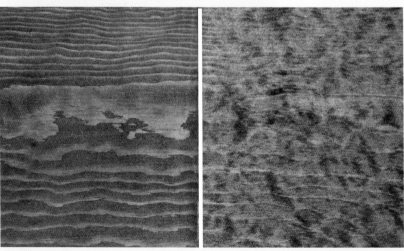

The easy way to eliminate blotching in pine is to use a gel stain (left half). This stain is so effective on pine that it should almost be called a "pine" stain.

Gel stain is less effective on tight-grained hardwoods such as cherry (left half). But the stain is still effective enough to make it a worthwhile choice over the difficult-to-control "wood conditioner."

Gel stain isn't for everything, however, because often you want deep penetration to highlight the wood's beauty. In this highly-figured wood, gel stain (LEFT) is clearly not a good choice when compared to oil stain (RIGHT).

## Gel Stains & Polyurethane; Difficulty: Low.

### WHAT IS IT?
An oil stain that has been thickened so it doesn't flow on its own.

### VARIATIONS
None

### THINS AND CLEANS UP WITH
Mineral spirits (paint thinner). Thinning with mineral spirits is not a good idea because it will destroy the flow-resistant properties, turning the stain into a liquid stain. If you want to thin a gel stain, use a clear gel varnish on "neutral" gel stain.

### HOW TO IDENTIFY
It is labeled "gel stain" and is thick in the can like mayonnaise.

### RULES FOR APPLICATION
- Wipe or brush a wet coat onto the wood.
- Wipe off the excess before the stain dries.

### WHEN TO USE
On any wood to change its color (darker, not lighter), but especially on blotch-prone pine and other softwoods, and on blotch-prone tight-grain hardwoods such as cherry, birch and maple.

### COMPATIBILITY
You can apply any finish over gel stain as long as the stain is dry. You can also apply gel stain over any finish (for example, to color in some dings and scratches), but you should then apply another coat of finish to keep the colorant from being rubbed off. All oil-based gel stains can be mixed to adjust the color.

### ADVANTAGES
- To avoid or reduce blotching in blotch-prone woods.
- To change the color of the wood.
- To make a cheaper or plainer wood look like a more expensive wood.

### DISADVANTAGES
- Deadens the richness of highly figured woods.
- Highlights flaws in wood, including mill marks (the tool marks left by the machines that mill the lumber), dents, gouges and scratches. You have to get these sanded out before applying the stain.
- Makes end grain darker unless it is sanded well.
- Dries rapidly.

### COMMON APPLICATION PROBLEMS
- Not getting all the stain wiped off before it dries.
- Highlighting of flaws in the wood.
- Highlighting of end grain.

## WHAT YOU NEED

(The following items are all available from a home center, paint store or woodworking store or catalog/website.)

- A pint or quart of gel stain.
- A pint or quart of oil-based polyurethane.
- A wide-mouth container.
- A pint or quart of mineral spirits.
- Protective gloves.
- A paintbrush. Best is a good quality that doesn't shed bristles. You could also use a foam brush or an inexpensive "chip" brush.
- Stirring sticks.
- A paint strainer.
- Sheets of #320- or #400-grit sandpaper.
- Lint-free rags such as old, clean T-shirts, cheese cloth or heavy duty paper towels.
- A tack rag (optional).
- A small brown paper bag.

## PREPARE THE STAIN

The thickness of gel stain usually prevents the pigment from settling to the bottom of the container, so shaking the stain is often all that is necessary for getting the stain ready to use. You can also stir the stain.

**1** Gel stain is similar to the consistency of mayonnaise. It resists dripping and running.

**2** Sometimes a little of the solvent in the gel stain rises to the top, so it's usually necessary to stir the stain, or at least shake the can.

## APPLY STAIN

Apply gel stain just like applying liquid oil stain — with a brush or rag. Keep in mind, however, that gel stain dries much faster than liquid oil stain, so you have to be fast if you use a brush. Usually, wiping the stain on the wood is best.

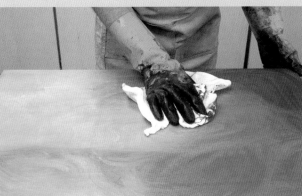

**3** (ABOVE LEFT) Gel stain is sometimes marketed for not dripping. I don't think this is the reason to use a gel stain. It's to reduce blotching, which is a characteristic of this birch panel.

**4** (ABOVE RIGHT) It's much faster to wipe stain onto wood than to brush it. But you can also brush the stain. Be aware, however, that gel stain dries much more rapidly than oil stain, so you need to get the stain on and wiped off fairly quickly.

**5** (LEFT) With the surface coated with the stain, wipe off the excess with a clean cloth. You can wipe in any direction, but it's usually a good idea to make your final wiping strokes go in the direction of the grain just in case you leave some streaks. They will be disguised by the grain.

## APPLY FINISH

After allowing the stain to dry overnight, brush on a finish as shown in the chapter on polyurethane.

**6** Begin brushing by depositing a brush load of the finish near the front edge of the panel.

**7** Then stretch the puddle of finish end to end. Continue across the surface, brushing each new brush stroke back into previous brush strokes.

# Water-based Finishes

Water-based finishes (sometimes called "waterborne" finishes) became available in the 1980s in response to the rising importance of developing finishes containing less polluting solvent. Essentially, clear water-based finish is latex paint without the pigment, so this finish isn't an entirely new product. And just as with latex paint, water-based finishes still contain some solvent, up to 20% in some cases.

Latex paint is more popular than oil paint because of reduced odor and easy soap-and-water clean up. Water-based finishes have the same low odor and easy clean up.

But because it's a finish rather than paint, some additional characteristics become important — specifically, water-based finishes raise the grain of the wood, dry fast and have no color. The grain raising and fast drying add to the difficulty applying the finish to wood. The lack of color stands out when compared to the yellow/orange coloring solvent-based finishes add to wood. The absence of color can be a positive in some cases and a negative in others.

You have to be alert when buying a water-based finish because manufacturers often don't distinguish them well from solvent-based finishes. Look for instructions to use water for clean up, and if you are still not sure, open the can. Water-based finishes appear white or off-white. (The white disappears when the finish dries.)

For this exercise/project you can use any brand of water-based finish, whether labeled "polyurethane," "varnish," "lacquer," "acrylic," "aqua," or whatever. The names don't correspond to any industry-standard differences, though you will experience some minor application differences among brands.

## Brushing Water-based Finish; Difficulty: Medium (Because It Dries So Fast)

### WHAT IS IT?

Water-based finish thins and cleans up with water but is resistant to water after it has dried. The finish is made with acrylic resin or a combination of acrylic and polyurethane resins. The combination is usually more durable. Neither type adds noticeable color to the wood (acrylic is the resin used to make Plexiglas). They only make the wood a little darker.

### VARIATIONS

Water-based finish varies in sheen (amount of gloss) depending on how much "flatting agent" is added. Common sheens are gloss, semi-gloss, satin, matte and flat. The sheen will be identified on the label, but there is no consistency among manufacturers about the meaning of each term.

### THINS AND CLEANS UP WITH
Water.

### HOW TO IDENTIFY
The product name and color of the label often reflect something to do with water, "clean," or environmental. Water is listed for clean up. The finish appears white in the can.

### RULES FOR APPLICATION
- Work rapidly because water-based finishes dry quickly, especially in hot, dry conditions.
- Brush back and forth in the direction of the wood grain, stretching the finish from end to end — just like painting.
- Watch what's happening in a reflected light, especially when brushing vertical surfaces, so you can see runs and sags as they develop and brush them out.
- Try to work in temperatures ranging between 65°F and 80°F for easiest application and best results.
- Allow several hours for drying in a warm room, garage or shop before applying another coat. The finish should be dry enough so it powders when sanded.

### WHEN TO USE
On any interior surface when you want reduced odor, easy clean up, or no color added to the wood. Be aware that water-based finishes aren't as water, scratch, heat or solvent resistant as oil-based finishes.

### COMPATIBILITY
- Works well over any water-based stain that contains a binder when the excess stain is wiped off.
- Oil-based stains should be allowed to dry thoroughly (up to a week

in a warm room) before applying water-based finish unless the labeling specifically says differently.
- Brushing will dissolve and drag dye color when no binder is included. Spray a coat of water-based aerosol to seal in the color before brushing.
- Can be applied over any paint or finish as long as it is dry, clean and dull. Wash to clean. Scuff with an abrasive pad to dull. The bond, however, is still not as good as can be achieved with solvent-based finishes.

### ADVANTAGES
- Low odor.
- Easy water, or soap-and-water, clean up.
- No color added to the wood. Looks especially nice on unstained "white" woods such as maple, birch and ash.
- Fast drying, so reduced dust nibs.

### DISADVANTAGES
- Raises the grain of the wood, making it feel rough.
- No color added to the wood. Darker woods, such as cherry, walnut and mahogany, look washed out unless a stain is applied.
- Fast drying, so greater difficulty brushing, especially on large surfaces.

### COMMON APPLICATION PROBLEMS
- Rough surface caused by grain raising and not sanding the first coat smooth.
- Runs and sags.
- Brush marks.

### WHAT YOU NEED
(The following items are all available from a home center, paint store or woodworking store or catalog/website.)
- A pint or quart of water-based finish—gloss or satin.
- A jar with a wide enough opening for the paintbrush to go through. (From your kitchen.)
- A two-inch-wide synthetic-bristle or foam paintbrush. Synthetic bristle is plastic (polyester or nylon) and specified for water-based or latex products.
- A paint strainer.
- A sheet of #220- or #320-grit sandpaper.
- A sanding block.
- Stirring sticks.
- Cloth rags.
- A small brown paper bag.

## PREPARE THE WATER-BASED FINISH

Straining is more important with water-based finishes than with other types of finish because of clumping and rust. Tiny clumps of finish often form in the finish, and rust develops around the lip of the can after it has been opened and closed several times.

**1** Stir the water-based finish to the bottom of the can if you are using anything but gloss. It's not necessary (but doesn't hurt anything) to stir gloss.

**2** Pour approximately the amount of finish you will need through a paint strainer into a jar with an opening larger than the width of your brush. You could use a coffee can, but you can't store the finish in the can because of rust. Working out of a separate container protects the original supply from dust or dirt you may pick up with your brush — especially likely with the first coat.

## BRUSHES

Water causes natural bristles to become limp and ineffective, so you should always use brushes with synthetic bristles when brushing water-based finishes. These brushes can be used with other finishes as well.

(LEFT) One way to identify brushes meant for water-based coatings is to look for a clue on the brush wrapper. It's obvious that these brushes will work fine. (RIGHT) Another way to identify brushes meant for water-based finishes is to find a description of the bristles used — often printed into the brush handle. There are two types of bristles used: nylon and polyester. Nylon is softer. Polyester is stiffer. Often the two types are mixed to create something in between. All work well, but knowing the difference may help you determine a favorite.

## FIRST COAT

If you are staining the wood, do so before applying the first coat of water-based finish. Water-based finishes dry rapidly, so they are much more difficult to brush onto a large surface than oil-based finishes. You need to move rapidly but in control.

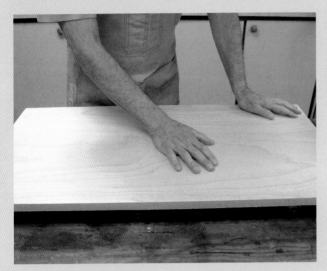

**1** Use your hand to wipe over the entire surface you are getting ready to brush to be sure the wood is clean. If dirty, vacuum (ideally) or blow or brush off the dust with compressed air or a dust brush. Blowing or brushing kicks dust into the air, and it will settle back on your newly applied finish. So you should do this in another location, then bring the panel back to the finishing area. Wipe over with your hand again, and wipe off the little dust your hand picks up onto your pants leg.

**2** On large horizontal surfaces the efficient way to apply a finish with a brush is to lift a brush load of finish out of the container and deposit it onto the surface. A brush load is finish about half way up the bristles, not all the way up to the metal. There's no point in tapping the brush against the side of the container or dragging the brush over the lip of the container unless you want to remove some of the finish so it doesn't drip. If you hold the container near where you intend to deposit the finish, dripping won't matter because you'll brush it out, and you will get the maximum amount of finish transferred. You could even pour some finish onto the surface and spread it with your brush.

**3** With some finish deposited in the middle of the area you intend to brush, spread or "stretch" the finish end-to-end by brushing back and fourth. If there isn't enough finish to create wetness end-to-end, deposit more.

**4** To keep from dragging your brush over the edge and creating runs, bring the brush down onto the surface in an airplane landing motion near the edge and move the brush across the surface and off the far edge. Make two or three strokes this way to line up brush strokes and knock off bubbles that might have been caused by the brushing.

**5** With the first brush load brushed end-to-end, deposit another brush load within an inch or so of the previous strokes and stretch it end-to-end and back into the first brushed area so it all appears as one. It's important to get this second (and continuing) brush strokes laid down and brushed back into the previous strokes before they begin setting up. This is called "keeping a wet edge." If the already brushed area is beginning to set up, the brush will drag this finish and create severe brush marks, which you will have to sand out after the finish has dried. Continue brushing across the surface, keeping a wet edge between strokes, until you have covered it all.

## TIP: Storing Brushes

If you want to use the same brush again within several days, you can avoid cleaning it if you wrap it tightly in plastic wrap so no air can get in, or scrunch the bristles against the bottom of a jar of water, then hang the brush in the jar with the water covering at least a quarter way up the bristles. Notice the extra hole I drilled in the brush handle so the brush hangs with its bristles not touching the bottom of the jar. If the bristles rest on the bottom, they may become permanently bent.

## SANDING BETWEEN COATS

The water part of water-based finishes swells wood grain causing it to "raise" and make the wood feel rough — much rougher than with solvent-based finishes. You could wet the wood, let it dry, then sand it smooth so the first coat of finish doesn't raise the grain so much. But it's easier just to sand the first coat.

**6** The first coat of water-based finish will usually dry in two or three hours unless it's very humid. You'll notice that the wood now feels very rough. It's critical for good results that you sand this first coat smooth.

**7** Sand the wood in the direction of the grain with a grit sandpaper that cuts off the roughness efficiently but doesn't create larger scratches than necessary. Usually, this is #220- or #320-grit sandpaper. In other words, try the #320 grit and if it requires a lot of sanding to make the surface feel smooth, switch to #220 grit. The coarser the grit sandpaper you use the more likely you are to sand through, and this will cause big problems if you have stained the wood. There's no reason to use a flat block to back the sandpaper. Your hand will do. Make two or three passes, then feel the wood to determine your progress. Your goal is simply to make the surface feel smooth.

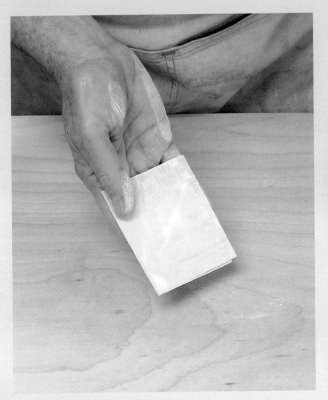

**8** The finish should powder on the sandpaper. If the finish doesn't powder, it isn't dry enough.

**9** When you are satisfied that the finish is smooth, clean off the sanding dust with a vacuum (best), compressed air or a dust brush. Then wipe the surface with a cloth lightly dampened with water. Don't use a tack rag because it will leave an oily residue that will interfere with the flow out and bonding of the next coat. The water won't raise the grain again because the wood is protected by the first coat.

## MORE COATS

For good results you always need to apply at least two coats. It's the second coat that produces the pleasing sheen, especially after you have sanded the first coat smooth.

**10** Just before applying each subsequent coat (two or three is usually adequate), wipe the surface with your hand to check that no dust has settled. Remove settled dust by wiping your hand on your pants leg.

**11** Apply this coat just as you applied the first. Deposit a brush load of finish onto the center of the near edge. Then stretch the finish end-to-end using airplane landing motions near the edges. Continue across the surface, working each newly applied stroke back into the previous strokes. Work fast enough to always keep a wet edge.

**12** Always watch what is happening in a reflected light so you can see problems, such as puddles, runs, dirt or bristles that may fall out, as they occur and fix them. If you mess things up really bad, you can wash off the finish with a wet rag if you're quick enough, or you can let the finish dry and sand out the problem. Brush marks always appear much worse just after application. They tend to level when the finish dries.

## BRUSH MARKS

Besides the grain raising, the biggest difficulty brushing water-based finish is caused by the rapid drying. If you aren't quick enough, the finish will begin setting up, and brushing over it will result in noticeable brush marks that stay in the finish.

**1** The fast drying helps reduce dust nibs, but it makes avoiding brush marks difficult on large surfaces. Try to get the finish on and spread end-to-end as rapidly as you can while still maintaining control. The marks shown here are from the area of the panel that I was showing in reflected light. I spent too much time brushing back over the same area while taking four or five photos.

**2** As long as you don't linger too long brushing over an area, water-based finishes usually level out well, as you can see in this photo from the middle of the panel. There aren't any visible brush marks.

**3** The only way to get rid of the brush marks is to sand them out after the finish has dried. Use a flat block to back your sandpaper so you cut the finish back evenly. Then apply another coat.

## VERTICAL AND COMPLEX

Objects other than flat, horizontal surfaces can be difficult to brush. Plan your order of brushing before starting, always brushing the most important parts last.

**1** When brushing vertical and complex surfaces, you need to remove some of the water-based finish from the brush before brushing. Do this either by dragging the bristles across the lip of the container or tapping the bristles against the inside of the container.

**2** If you try to brush a narrow spindle or edge, the bristles on the brush will probably separate. So, brush across the grain, or better, at an angle to the grain.

**3** Many brands of water-based finish run easily on vertical surfaces. Always watch what is happening in a reflected light (overhead light, window or light on a stand) and brush out any runs or sags as they develop. If you've got too much finish on the wood, use your brush to transfer some of the excess to a non-brushed area or back into the container.

## FINISH UP

(BELOW) After two or three coats, when the finish looks good, you are finished. But there is one more trick you can use to improve your results. If there are small dust nibs in the last coat of finish, you can usually remove them and make the surface feel smoother by rubbing with a brown paper bag after the finish has dried for a couple of days.

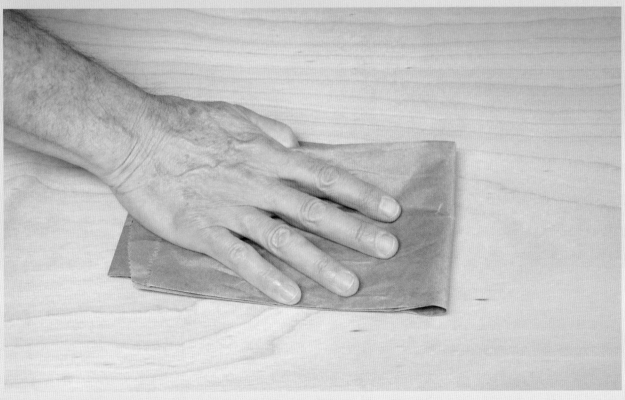

Think of water-based stain as thinned latex paint. The only important difference, in fact, is the colors available. There's no reason you couldn't thin a latex paint with water and apply it as a stain.

Water-based stains are the most difficult stains to use because they dry so fast, especially in hot, dry conditions. So you have to work fast, work on smaller areas at a time or get a second person to wipe off soon after you apply.

Otherwise, water-based stains resemble oil stains in the appearance they produce, and water-based stains are the best stains to use under a water-based finish.

## Applying Water-based Stain; Difficulty: Medium

### WHAT IS IT?

A stain is a colorant (pigment or dye) added to a little finish and a lot of thinner. In the case of water-based stains the finish is water-based finish, which you can think of as latex paint without the pigment. As with oil-based stains, water-based stains are sometimes called "wiping" stains or "pigment" stains.

### VARIATIONS

None.

### THINS AND CLEANS UP WITH

Water.

### HOW TO IDENTIFY

Any liquid stain that thins and cleans up with water.

### RULES FOR APPLICATION
- Wipe, brush or spray onto the wood.
- Wipe off all or most of the excess before the stain dries.

### WHEN TO USE

On any wood to change its color (darker, not lighter) and add definition (depth) to the grain.

### COMPATIBILITY

You can apply any finish over water-based stain as long as the stain is dry. You can also apply water-based stain over any finish (for example, to color in some dings and scratches), but you need to work fast or on small areas to give yourself enough time to get all the stain wiped off the areas you don't want it (leaving it just in the dings and scratches, for example). All stains that thin with water can be mixed to adjust the color.

### ADVANTAGES
- To change the color of the wood.
- To make a cheaper or plainer wood look like a more expensive wood.
- To make a darker wood such as cherry or walnut appear richer under a water-based finish. These finishes tend to make darker woods look "washed-out" if no stain is applied.

- Water-based stain doesn't highlight blotching in woods such as pine and cherry nearly as much as does oil stain and dye stain.
- To avoid the use of the much larger amount of solvent in oil stains.
- For easier water clean up.
- When the excess is wiped off, water-based stain accentuates the grain of the wood making it look deeper and usually richer.

## DISADVANTAGES

- Stain highlights the flaws in wood, including mill marks (the tool marks left by the machines that milled the lumber), dents, gouges and scratches. You have to get these sanded out before applying the stain. (See the chapter on preparing wood.)
- Dries fast, especially in hot and dry conditions, and this makes application difficult on large surfaces.
- Raises the grain of the wood.

## COMMON APPLICATION PROBLEMS

- Highlighting of flaws such as mill marks, dents, gouges and scratches.
- Streaks, lap marks and blotching because you didn't get the stain wiped off before it dried in places.

## MAKE YOUR OWN

You can make your own water-based stain in two ways: thin a latex paint with water, or add universal colorant (the colorant paint stores add to latex paint to tint it) to a water-based finish and thin it with water.

## WHAT YOU NEED

(The following items are all available from a home center, paint store or woodworking store or catalog/website.)

- A pint or quart of water-based stain.
- A pint or quart of water-based finish.
- A wide-mouth jar.
- Latex or other protective gloves.
- Stirring sticks.
- A synthetic (nylon or polyester) bristle brush and possibly a foam brush.
- Lint-free rags such as old, clean T-shirts, cheesecloth or heavy-duty paper towels.
- A paint strainer.
- Sheets of #220- and #320-grit sandpaper.
- A sanding block.
- An abrasive pad.
- A small brown paper bag.

## PREPARE THE STAIN

Most water-based stains contain pigment, which settles to the bottom of the can. You have to stir it into suspension before applying the stain.

**1** If a stain has sat undisturbed on a shelf for a while, all the pigment will have settled to the bottom. You can lift it with a stirring stick.

**2** Always stir the stain before each use. Pigment can lump hard enough on the bottom of the can to make hand shaking ineffective.

## APPLY STAIN

Water-based stains dry rapidly, which can make staining large surfaces difficult. Divide the project into smaller parts or sections if you can, or get a second person to wipe off after you apply.

**3** Wipe a wet coat of stain onto the entire surface. You can wipe in any direction or in circles. You can speed the process on horizontal surfaces by pouring on the stain and spreading it with a cloth. For vertical surfaces, get the cloth soaking wet and spread the stain. You can also brush the stain, of course, but it is much slower and you are much more likely not to get everything covered and wiped off before the stain starts to dry.

**4** You're not going to know how much time you have, of course, until you actually use the stain. Water-based stains vary a little in drying time, but the weather is the big factor with hot and dry making application the most difficult. So, consider staining a practice object before committing to the project. The object can be scrap plywood or simply a large cardboard box. Here, the stain has dried too hard to get it wiped off.

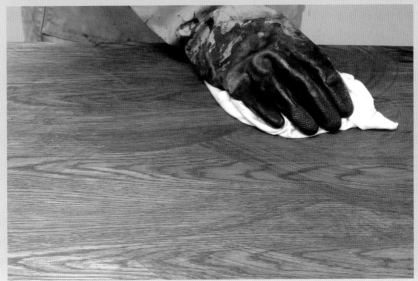

**5** (BELOW LEFT AND RIGHT) If you have a situation where the stain dries on you before you can get it wiped off, quickly apply more stain. It will soften what is there making it easier to wipe off.

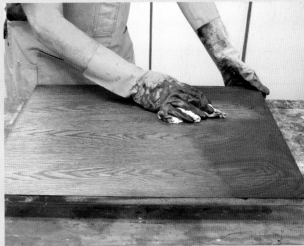

**6** If you aren't quick enough, you may still have a problem getting the streaks out. To help, scrub the surface while it's wet with stain using an abrasive pad (RIGHT). Don't use steel wool; shards that break off will rust. Then wipe off the excess quickly (MIDDLE RIGHT).

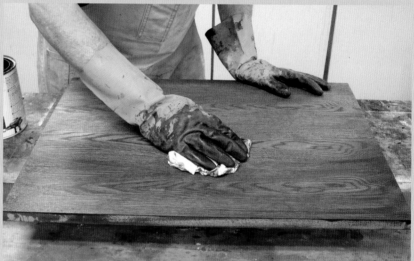

**7** If you don't have any abrasive pads handy, you can use a Scotch-Brite scrub pad from the kitchen. It's a little coarse, so don't scrub too hard with it or you'll begin removing color from the wood and lose control. If everything fails, you'll have to strip the stain with a strong solvent such as lacquer thinner or acetone, or with a paint stripper. Get the remaining color as even as you can, then apply the stain again, working faster, on smaller sections as a time, or with the help of someone else.

## APPLYING WATER-BASED FINISH

The water-based stain will raise the grain making the wood feel rough. Don't sand it; you'll sand to different depths and lose control of the color. Instead, apply the first coat of finish. In other words, "bury" the raised grain. Let the finish dry, then sand the raised grain smooth with #220-grit or #320-grit sandpaper. Be careful not to sand through to the stain.

**1** (RIGHT) On flat horizontal surfaces begin by depositing a brush load of finish in the middle of the near edge.

**2** (BELOW LEFT AND RIGHT) Stretch the deposited finish end-to-end.

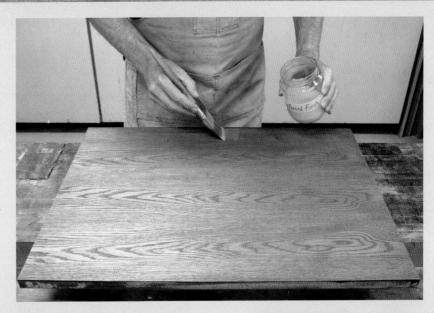

**3** Then deposit additional brush loads about an inch beyond the previously brushed area and stretch them end-to-end and back into the previously brushed areas. Work across the surface in this manner, always "keeping a wet edge."

# Solvents and Thinners

Finishing can't exist without solvents and thinners — even water-based stains and finishes contain them. If you understand a little about solvents and how they relate to one another, you'll have more control of your work. You'll be able to speed up or slow down the drying time of your finish to compensate for the weather, and you'll be able to manipulate the viscosity of your finish to make it flow better. You'll also be better able to choose the best solvent for cleaning in various situations.

Though the terms "solvent" and "thinner" often are used interchangeably (and I will sometimes use the more general term "solvent" here to refer to both), they are actually quite different. A solvent is a liquid that dissolves a solid, such as a cured finish, while a thinner is a liquid that thins a stain or finish already in liquid form. Sometimes a liquid solvent or thinner just thins a finish, and other times it both dissolves and thins a finish.

Solvents are grouped in families. There are five families, not including the special ones used in paint-and-varnish removers: petroleum distillates, alcohols, ketones, esters and glycol ethers. Each family reacts with a finish in a different way.

Within each family, solvents differ primarily in evaporation rate, with some evaporating rapidly at room temperature and others evaporating very slowly or not at all.

Here's the easy way to understand solvents for wood finishes.

First, divide the solvents between the petroleum distillates, including turpentine, and all the rest. Because most of the solvents on the shelves are petroleum distillates, this reduces the rest to a number that's easy to handle.

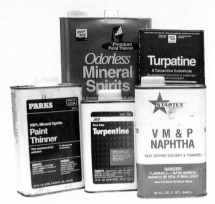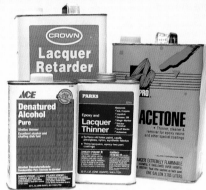

The easy way to makes sense of solvents is to divide them into petroleum distillates (LEFT) and all the others (RIGHT). Once you understand the petroleum distillates, all do essentially the same thing at different evaporation rates, it's easy to handle the rest.

Then make sense of the petroleum distillates and turpentine, all of which do essentially the same thing at different evaporation rates, and when this is done, deal with the rest.

## PETROLEUM DISTILLATES

Petroleum distillates are all distillations of petroleum. They include mineral spirits (paint thinner), naphtha, toluene, xylene and some "turpentine substitutes" such as turpatine and T.R.P.S. The primary use for these solvents in wood finishing is thinning waxes, oils and varnishes, including polyurethane varnish, and cleaning brushes. The solvents are also used to clean oil, grease and wax.

Turpentine is a distillation of pine tree sap. Before the mid-20th century, turpentine was widely used as a thinner and clean-up solvent for oil paint and varnish and also as a grease and wax cleaner.

With the growth of the automobile industry and its need for petroleum products, a large number of petroleum solvents were introduced and these have almost entirely replaced turpentine because they are less expensive and have less unpleasant odor. The only sector in which turpentine is still used in any significant quantity is fine arts.

To distill petroleum, it is heated higher and higher and the gases released at different temperatures are condensed into the various liquid solvents.

The first gas to come off is methane, which doesn't condense at room temperature, only at much colder temperatures. Then there's ethane, propane, butane, etc. Heptane and octane are used to make gasoline, a liquid that evaporates very rapidly. Gasoline is sometimes used as a cleaner, but it is very dangerous because it is explosive. About 20 years ago the retired local sheriff in my town, an amateur woodworker, died of burns he received in an explosion while using gasoline for cleaning.

The solvents we use in wood finishing evaporate much more slowly than gasoline and are relatively safe to use, even with poor ventilation. But it's still unwise to use them in a room with a flame such as a pilot light.

Kerosene is also widely available, but it evaporates too slowly to be of much use in finishing. Mineral oil (also called paraffin oil) and paraffin wax don't evaporate at all at room temperature. Paraffin wax, in fact, is a solid at room temperature.

You may have noticed in using these solvents that the slower the evaporation, the oilier the liquid substance. Mineral spirits is oilier than naphtha, and kerosene is oilier than mineral spirits. Mineral oil is oil. Because none of these distillations damage finishes (except wax), and because oily substances are effective at picking up dust and adding shine to dull surfaces, petroleum distillates are widely used as the main ingredient in furniture polishes.

## MINERAL SPIRITS & NAPHTHA

The two most widely used finishing solvents are mineral spirits and naphtha. For our purposes, the principal differences between the two are evaporation rate and oiliness. Naphtha evaporates more quickly than mineral spirits and is "drier," that is, less oily. Naphtha is therefore better for cleaning all types of oily, greasy or waxy surfaces. Mineral spirits is better for thinning oils, varnishes (including polyurethane varnish) and oil-based paints because it leaves more time for the coating to level after brushing.

Naphtha is a stronger solvent than mineral spirits, but this is rarely significant in wood finishing. Mineral spirits is strong enough for any normal operation.

To better place turpentine among the petroleum distillates, think of it as having the solvent strength of naphtha but the evaporation rate and oiliness of mineral spirits. I don't know of any situation in wood finishing where this is important.

The nickname for mineral spirits is "paint thinner." Back in the early days of mineral spirits, before World War II, all paints were oil-based. So there was only one thinner for paint. The nickname made sense.

Today, with water-based paints and finishes in wide use, the name could be confusing to beginners. Paint thinner is used only with oil-based paints and finishes.

It's important to emphasize that mineral spirits and paint thinner are the same thing. Amazingly, there are manufacturers who try to trick you into paying more by labeling their containers "pure" mineral spirits and charging more.

The common naphtha available in paint stores is VM&P Naphtha. VM&P stands for "varnish makers and painters." Stronger and faster evaporating naphthas exist, but these are rarely sold to the general public.

## TOLUENE & XYLENE

Toluene, nicknamed "toluol," and xylene, nicknamed "xylol," are the strong, smelly, fast-evaporating and "dry" parts of mineral spirits and naphtha. These solvents are removed from mineral spirits and naphtha at refineries and sold separately as cleaners, and also as solvents for some high-performance spray finishes such as conversion varnish. Toluene and xylene are very effective as cleaners, but I find naphtha adequate for almost all situations.

Toluene evaporates a little more quickly than xylene, but this is significant only when using the solvent as a thinner.

Any petroleum distillate or turpentine can be used to thin wax, oil or varnish, but mineral spirits (paint thinner) is best. It gives the finish time to level and is less expensive and has less unpleasant odor than turpentine.

Naphtha is usually better than mineral spirits for cleaning oily or waxy surfaces (including crayon marks) because it evaporates much faster. Naphtha also has more solvent strength than mineral spirits, which is sometimes helpful on old waxed surfaces such as this one.

Toluene and xylene are very useful for removing latex paint spatter from all surfaces except water-based finishes. The commercial products Oops! and Goof Off are based on xylene and sold for this purpose.

Denatured alcohol is the best solvent for thinning shellac. It is much less toxic than methanol.

The problem with these two solvents is that they are relatively toxic. They will affect your nervous system causing irritability and drunkenness, and in large doses could cause serious health problems. You should never use them in any sizeable quantity in a room without good exhaust.

One very interesting use for toluene and xylene is to soften latex paint. Using a dampened cloth (and solvent-resistant gloves) you can easily remove latex paint that has spattered off a paint roller, or even a full coat of latex paint, from any finish except water-based finish, without causing any damage to the underlying finish. In fact, the products sold specifically to do this, "Oops!" and "Goof-Off," are principally xylene.

Because white and yellow glues are the same chemistry as latex paint, you can also use toluene or xylene to soften and scrub these glues from wood when you have glue seepage or fingerprints that you didn't fully remove during sanding. You will need to use a toothbrush or soft brass wire brush to get the glue out of the pores.

## ODORLESS MINERAL SPIRITS

The mineral spirits left after the toluene and xylene are removed is sold as "odorless" mineral spirits. When understood this way, it's obvious that odorless mineral spirits is a weaker solvent than regular mineral spirits. But I've never found this to be a problem. It still appears to be strong enough to thin all common oils, varnishes and oil paints.

The disadvantage of odorless mineral spirits, of course, is that it is considerably more expensive because of the extra steps necessary to produce it. You may find the extra expense worth it, however, just to avoid the unpleasant odor of regular mineral spirits.

## TURPENTINE SUBSTITUTES

The so-called turpentine substitutes are an interesting breed. My first question when I talk to the companies that produce them is, "Isn't that the role of mineral spirits?" (One company spokesman, identified as the "chemist," explained that these products were necessary because of all the protests against cutting down trees to make turpentine! Of course, trees aren't cut down; the sap is drained.)

Actually, these solvents seem to have similar characteristics to turpentine in that they have the solvent strength of naphtha but an evaporation rate closer to mineral spirits. So they are useful to

fine artists but provide no special benefit to wood finishers.

These are all of the petroleum distillates used in wood finishing. Now for the other solvents.

## ALCOHOL

Alcohol is the solvent for shellac. The solvent dissolves solid shellac flakes and thins the liquid shellac after dissolving. There are two alcohol types available at paint stores: methanol and denatured.

Methanol evaporates a little faster than denatured, but it is toxic and could blind or even kill you if you breathe too high a vapor concentration for too long. You shouldn't use it unless you have good ventilation in your shop.

Denatured alcohol is ethyl alcohol (the alcohol in beer, wine and liquor) that has been made poisonous so we don't have to pay liquor taxes to buy it. This is the alcohol you should use with shellac.

In situations where shellac is not the finish, alcohol has the further use as a felt-tip-pen ink remover. Dampen a cloth and wipe over the mark and you will remove it in most cases. You won't damage any finish except shellac as long as you don't soak the surface.

Denatured alcohol is especially useful for removing felt-tip-pen marks. The solvent won't damage any finish except shellac, as long as you don't soak the surface.

Lacquer thinner is a blend of half-a-dozen or so solvents specially formulated for thinning lacquer. The blend allows for differing evaporation rates and for evaporation in steps to reduce runs on vertical surfaces.

## LACQUER THINNER

Lacquer thinner is the solvent and thinner for all the types of lacquer, including nitrocellulose, CAB-acrylic and catalyzed. It's the most interesting of the solvents because it's composed of half-a-dozen or so different individual solvents. Manufacturers vary these to control solvent strength and evaporation rate.

Solvents from five different families are used in lacquer thinners, including toluene, xylene and "high-flash" (meaning fast evaporating) naphtha from the petroleum-distillate family. The other four families are ketones, esters, glycol ethers and alcohols.

All the individual solvents from the ketone, ester and glycol-ether families dissolve lacquer on their own, but they evaporate at different rates. So manufacturers choose among them to make a thinner that evaporates in steps at the speeds they want. Alcohol doesn't dissolve lacquer on its own, but it does when in combination with these other solvents. So one or more of the alcohols is usually added to the mix to reduce cost.

The nature of lacquer is that it can be fully dissolved and still be too thick to spray efficiently. So to further thin the lacquer without adding expensive dissolving solvents, manufacturers add up to 50 percent toluene, xylene or high-flash naphtha to, in effect, "thin" the lacquer thinner.

By varying the solvents used, manufacturers can control the strength of lacquer thinner (automotive lacquers need a higher percentage of dissolving solvent) and the speed of evaporation. For example, lacquer retarders are made to evaporate slower so the lacquer stays "open" on the surface of the wood longer in order to eliminate blushing (turning white) in humid weather and dry spray (a sandy surface) in hot weather.

The purpose of using multiple individual solvents evaporating at intervals is to control the thickening of the lacquer on a vertical surface to reduce runs. The lacquer thickens quickly after being sprayed but enough of the slower-evaporating solvents remain so the finish has time to flatten out. Lacquer thinner is unique among solvents for having this characteristic.

A cheaper "clean-up" lacquer thinner is often available. It's made with a higher percentage of "thinning" petroleum-distillate solvents and doesn't dissolve lacquer well. You will have problems if you use this thinner for thinning lacquer.

## BRUSH CLEANERS & DEGLOSSERS

Brands of brush cleaner and deglosser (liquid sandpaper) vary greatly in their composition. Some are even water-based, but these work more slowly and are less effective than solvent-based.

You can usually substitute a brush cleaner for the mineral spirits or lacquer thinner you may otherwise use to clean your varnish, lacquer or water-based finish brushes. (It's easiest to clean shellac with household ammonia and water.) Brush cleaners are usually more expensive, however.

What is left unsaid about deglossers is that it matters greatly which paint or finish you're trying to clean and dull. Cleaning grease or wax is no problem, but high-performance paints and finishes such as UV-cured coatings, catalyzed lacquer, conversion varnish and even oil-based polyurethane are very solvent resistant. So it's rarely possible to dull them short of abrading with real sandpaper or steel wool.

# Aerosol Finishing

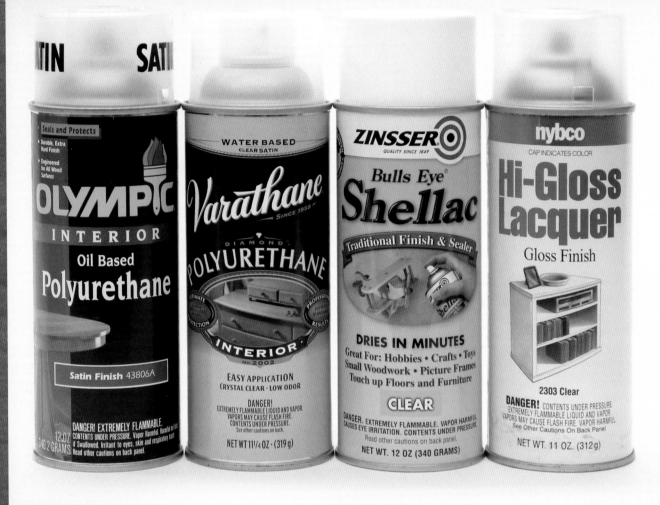

Common types of finishes sold in aerosol containers are from the left: oil-based polyurethane, water-based polyurethane, shellac and lacquer. These finishes are usually available in gloss, semi-gloss and satin sheen.

Wood finishes available in aerosol containers include oil-based polyurethane, water-based polyurethane, shellac and lacquer. The finishes in the containers are the same as those sold for brushing or spraying through a spray gun. With aerosols, however, the finish is thinned more, so it fits easily through the small hole in the nozzle. As a result, you have to spray more coats using an aerosol to get the same film thickness on the wood.

Because of the packaging, aerosol finishes are more expensive than finishes sold in cans. But aerosols are capable of producing the same level surface as can be achieved with a spray gun, and they do so with similar speed and without the equipment expense and tuning and cleaning difficulties required with spray guns.

It's important to point out that chlorofluorocarbons (CFCs), which damage the upper ozone layer, have not been used in aerosols containing wood finishes since 1978. Instead, liquefied petroleum gases (LPGs), such as propane, are used to propel the liquid finish through the nozzle.

# Aerosol Finishing; Difficulty: Low.

## WHAT IS IT?
Any type of finish packaged in an aerosol container and sprayed like a spray gun.

## RULES FOR APPLICATION
- Spray evenly-thick coats on the wood.
- Watch what is happening in a reflected light so you get an evenly-wet coat without runs or sags on vertical surfaces.
- Allow each coat to dry thoroughly before spraying the next.
- Sand lightly between each coat — especially important after the first coat — to make the surface feel smooth.

## WHEN TO USE
On any surface. You are choosing the type of finish to use. The aerosol is merely the packaging for the finish.

## COMPATIBILITY
It's the finish you're using not the aerosol that determines compatibility. See the chapters on oil-based polyurethane and water-based finish.

## ADVANTAGES
- Very easy to use.
- Produces a level surface without brush marks.
- Faster than brushing.

## DISADVANTAGES
- More expensive than brushing because of the added expense of the aerosol container and waste from all the finish that misses the target.

## COMMON APPLICATION PROBLEMS
- Dust nibs, especially with slower drying oil-based polyurethane and water-based polyurethane.
- Runs and sags on vertical surfaces.
- Uneven spray from the container because your finger is draping over the exit hole in the nozzle, or finish has dried in the nozzle blocking part of it.

## NOZZLE DIFFERENCES
There are many types of nozzles made for aerosols but only two are used with wood finishes: cone-shaped and fan-shaped.

The most common nozzle used on aerosols containing a wood finish produces a cone-shaped spray pattern. You have no control over the pattern.

Some brands of finish use a nozzle that produces a fan-shaped spray pattern, just like a spray gun. This nozzle can be adjusted to spray a vertical or horizontal fan pattern by using pliers to rotate the small rectangular disk on the front of the nozzle. The aerosols with these nozzles lay down a more even finish than aerosols with the cone-shaped pattern.

## OPERATING AN AEROSOL

Aerosols are everywhere in our society and everyone knows how to use them. Here are some tips for using aerosols containing wood finishes.

**1** To operate an aerosol, point the hole in the nozzle towards the target and press down on the nozzle with your finger. Be careful to keep your finger just on the top so it doesn't drape over the front edge and interfere with the spray.

**2** Trigger units for aerosol cans are available at most stores and catalogues that sell aerosols. These units are inexpensive, fit all aerosols and make application much less taxing on your index finger when spraying large surfaces.

**3** When you have finished a spraying session and there's still finish in the container, clean the nozzle and the interior tube by turning the aerosol upside down and spraying until no more finish comes out, just propellant. Then wipe the nozzle dry with a cloth or paper towel. If you don't do this, the finish could harden in the nozzle and ruin the aerosol for any future use. You're wasting money by skipping the cleaning step.

## SPRAYING PROCEDURE

The rules for aerosol spraying are the same as for spraying with a spray gun. The idea is to spray a roughly even thickness of finish everywhere.

**1** For large flat surfaces, begin spraying with the spray half on and half off one edge.

**2** Continue across the surface by overlapping each spraying pass by half until you reach the opposite edge. Spray this last pass half on and half off. After the finish dries, sand it lightly with #320- or #400-grit sandpaper, clean off the dust, and spray another coat. Sanding is especially important after the first coat to make the surface feels smooth. You can apply as many coats as you want — until you have achieved a pleasing look. Don't sand the last coat.

# Antiques Roadshow and the Deterioration of Furniture

One of the most watched PBS programs is the "Antiques Roadshow," which has been broadcast since 1996. The format features some of our nation's foremost antiques experts and appraisers explaining to a nationwide audience the monetary value and some of the history of the objects shown. These objects include almost everything you can think of that is old or antique, ranging in size from jewelry to large pieces of furniture. (As applied to furniture, the term "antique" is variously defined as at least 100 years old or pre-industrial, which usually means 1840s or earlier. So I'm using the phrase "old or antique" to be sure to include everything that might appear on the show.)

The "Roadshow" tours a dozen or so cities each year, bringing many of its stable of about 150 appraisers to each. (The appraisers work without pay and cover their own expenses; side benefits created by the national television exposure usually give back many times over.) Thousands of people line up at each venue to have two or more objects appraised. The most interesting appraisals are filmed for later use on the television broadcast.

The format of the "Roadshow" is very entertaining. The show could stand on its own just for this quality. But it has another very important enticement: It appeals to the "win-the-lottery" fantasy of most people. In the majority of cases, the people shown on the "Roadshow" are pleasantly surprised and often elated to learn that their object is worth far more than they thought — often in the thousands of dollars. Maybe there's also something in the viewer's attic that is worth a lot of money? Maybe the viewer will find that he or she has "won

Rarely should old painted furniture be stripped, no matter how deteriorated the paint, because unlike clear-finished furniture, it's the paint itself, rather than the design or construction, that provides almost all the character and value. This painted blanket chest would lose all its interest and value if it were stripped.

the lottery" with what was previously thought to be junk.

The "Roadshow" is also educational. I know many professional refinishers and antique dealers who watch to learn. But most (and maybe all) complain about the misleading message that is being sent concerning furniture. It's the pivotal message of the entire show, the

message everyone associates with the "Antiques Roadshow": "Don't refinish!" Refinishing reduces the value of furniture, it is alleged, sometimes by thousands of dollars.

It's my contention that this message misleads the public about the appropriateness (or inappropriateness) of refinishing. The message indirectly causes

Light destroys finishes. Direct sunlight and fluorescent light are the most damaging. The backside of this walnut cabinet sat next to a west-facing window for 10 years. The finish is peeling and the color is faded where the sunlight hit.

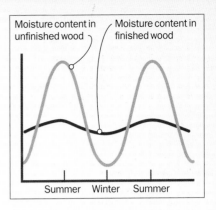

A finish in good condition reduces the swelling and shrinking of wood by slowing the exchange of moisture in and out of wood. This graph represents a hypothetical situation.

serious damage to old and antique furniture and will result in the disappearance of much of it unless the message is changed.

Furniture requires a finish in good shape to protect the wood from moisture exchange and to make the wood look nice. Furniture with joint failure, peeling veneer, warps and splits — all caused by excessive moisture exchange — and furniture that looks bad because of a deteriorated and ugly finish, often ends up in an attic, basement, garage or barn where it further deteriorates. Or it is tossed out.

## HOW FURNITURE DETERIORATES

Furniture deteriorates as a result of exposure to moisture, light and abuse.

Moisture affects the wood. Contact with water and changes in humidity cause wood to expand and contract across the grain, but not significantly along the grain. When boards are joined perpendicularly, as they almost always are to make furniture, stress develops in the joints because of contrary wood movement in the parts. As the glue ages and becomes brittle, this stress causes the glue to give way. The joints then loosen and separate.

The same happens with veneer, which was often glued perpendicularly to a solid-wood substrate or laid over a frame-and-flush-panel substrate. The veneer separates or cracks, especially over the joints.

Exposure of only one side of wood to water also causes warping and splitting, a poorly understood phenomenon, which I explain in "Tabletops & the Need to Refinish" at the end of this chapter.

Moisture-vapor exchange (higher humidity in the air leading to higher moisture content in the wood, and vice versa) has always been a problem. But it has become worse in modern, tightly constructed buildings because of the impact of central heating. In the winter, interior humidity conditions become much drier than previously, so the variations between summer and winter are greater. The result is increased wood movement.

The easiest way to keep moisture exchange to a minimum is to keep the finish in good shape. (The other way is to maintain a constant humidity, which is usually not possible outside of a museum setting.) A finish doesn't completely stop moisture penetration, but it slows the penetration significantly. A deteriorated finish is pitted with microscopic voids that allow moisture in liquid or vapor form to pass through. An old, deteriorated finish offers almost no barrier to moisture penetration.

While the deterioration of the wood in furniture is caused primarily by moisture exchange, the deterioration of finishes results primarily from exposure to light.

A finish will eventually dull, become brittle and crack simply because of exposure to oxygen, but this takes a very long time. Exposure to ultraviolet light, especially from sunlight and fluorescent lighting, accelerates this deterioration considerably. The finish on a piece of furniture placed near a window in direct sunlight will dull and crack far sooner than a finish placed in a dark corner across the room.

Finishes can also deteriorate from abuse, of course. Abuse in the form of scratches and rubs removes finishes and may even damage the wood.

No matter how a finish deteriorates, the end result is increased moisture exchange in the wood, reduced functionality and increased ugliness. And, with rare exceptions, this deterioration leads eventually to the disappearance of the furniture if nothing is done to reverse it.

## THE MISLEADING MESSAGE

Some very old furniture has survived in good condition, but the instances of this happening are rare. The furniture that has done so, however, is worth more than furniture that has had to be refinished. People will pay more for things that are rare.

How does some furniture survive for hundreds of years with its original finish in good condition? Consider this scenario as an example.

A bureau (chest-of-drawers) is made for a wealthy New England family in

The decision of whether to refinish, rejuvenate or leave alone varies with each piece of furniture (and also with the desires of the owner). At right is an early 19th-century bow front bureau with a badly damaged finish, including significant missing color. As is, the piece is very unattractive. The choice would probably be to refinish, or possibly to rejuvenate using the amalgamation technique, hoping to move some of the color around to fill in. (Nothing would be lost if amalgamation didn't produce good results because refinishing is the other choice; it could still be done.) On the right is the arm of a painted Windsor chair from about the same period, with clear patterns of wear. It would be a shame to remove, or try to amalgamate and respread, the paint. The wear adds to the character and value.

1790. It is used by that family for a couple decades then passed down to one of the children who remains in the family house. But the bureau is no longer "modern" and is relegated to a dark corner in a guest bedroom where it is rarely used. The house and bureau remain in the family for 200 years, after which the bureau is sold and enters the antiques market with a finish that is a little dull but otherwise in near-original condition.

The circumstances necessary for furniture to survive in near-original condition are that it receive little exposure to bright light and be rarely used or moved.

As chance would have it, the furniture appraisers who appear on the "Roadshow" deal primarily with this type of furniture in their own businesses. There is a small but very enthusiastic market for furniture with old or original "surfaces." It is therefore natural for these appraisers to compare the value of an object that has been refinished with one that hasn't. Had the furniture survived in near-original condition, it would be worth much more.

But I rarely hear the appraisers explain survivability on the "Roadshow." Instead, they say things like, "Had this furniture not been refinished, it would be worth many thousands of dollars. But it was refinished, so now it's worth only a few thousand dollars."

To the unsophisticated viewer this evaluation says, "Furniture loses value when it is refinished."

It's rarely explained that furniture is seldom refinished unless it needs to be. And if the furniture needs to be refinished and it isn't, it may not survive. The appraisers should be saying, "This piece was refinished, which is good because it surely needed to be. In this condition, it's worth "X" dollars. Had it been one of those rare pieces of furniture that survived with its original finish in good condition, it would be worth this much more. You should be happy that someone cared enough to refinish the furniture so you have the opportunity to enjoy it."

Or, in cases of badly deteriorated finishes on pieces with no special provenance, the appraisers should say something like, "The finish on this piece is in very poor condition and is no longer serving its protective purpose. The furniture would be worth more refinished."

As chance would also have it, most of the leading museums in the country have an interest in keeping furniture in their collections in the same condition as when it was acquired — often with a very deteriorated finish. (Museums spend a lot of effort controlling humidity.) The purpose is so the furniture can be studied for original techniques, adhesives and finishes used.

Therefore, when a museum curator or conservator is asked by a consumer magazine to comment on the appropriateness of refinishing, the response is almost always, "Refinishing is bad." The museum professional is thinking of his or her own needs, not those of the general public. The result is that the "Roadshow's" message is reinforced.

More sophisticated dealers and collectors don't object to refinishing. The market for old and antique furniture in deteriorated condition is very small. Most people want their furniture to look good, which usually means refinished, or at least restored as I describe below in "Rejuvenating Old Finishes." This has been brought home to me on a number of occasions when I've visited high-end antique stores, especially in the Northeast. I've walked through shops containing hundreds of pieces of furniture from the late 18th and early 19th centuries, every one of which has been refinished at some point in its life, usually fairly recently.

The shop owners explain to me that there isn't a market for "crusty craze." People want their furniture to look nice. Or as one dealer at one of the most prestigious New York City stores said when I asked about the influence of the "Antiques Roadshow": "Our customers know better."

## THE OTHER SIDE

There's another side to this issue. An old or original finish makes it easier to determine the authenticity of a small percentage of antique furniture. There are fakes and restorations at all levels of the market, and crusty old finishes, which are difficult if not impossible to replicate, provide a high degree of insurance against fraud. Even old dirt in cracks and recesses is helpful. An original or at least very old finish makes authentication easier and sales better for a few high-end dealers.

This desire for old, deteriorated and even dirty surfaces could be consciously or unconsciously motivating the appraisers on the "Roadshow."

It could well be argued that this is fair, that there is a legitimate authentication rationale for not refinishing no matter how bad the condition of the finish. But even if you accept this rationale, it doesn't apply to the vast majority (somewhere north of 99 percent) of old and antique furniture. The mantra, "Don't refinish," should not be promoted on a television show targeted at the general public without constant explaining. The current practice is having a harmful effect.

# Rejuvenating Old Finishes

There are three ways to deal with an old, deteriorated finish: You can leave it as is, doing no more than possibly apply some paste wax; you can strip and refinish; or you can rejuvenate or "restore" whatever finish is left. The decision is always made on a case-by-case basis. No method is right for all furniture.

In many cases, an old finish surface has an attractive aged coloring that will be lost if the finish is stripped and a new one applied. Refinishing makes furniture look new and can cause it to lose some of its charm. On the other hand, if the finish is unattractive and no longer performing its function of slowing moisture exchange, something should be done. There are a number of techniques you can use to rejuvenate an old finish that will maintain the color while at the same time improve the overall appearance. Here is a list of techniques, advancing from least to most intrusive, effective and difficult to pull off.

- Apply a commercial "restorer," such as Howard's Restor-A-Finish. This will add shine, and sometimes color, to scratches for a short time.
- Apply paste wax. Wax will add a semi-permanent shine without highlighting cracks in the finish (as liquid polishes do). But wax won't improve resistance to moisture exchange in any significant way. Use a colored paste wax to add color in scratches and dings.
- Clean the surface with soap and water and/or mineral spirits before applying wax or a restorer. There are two types of dirt, water-soluble and solvent-soluble, so you may need to use both types of cleaner.
- Apply a coat or two of finish. You can use any finish, including shellac, varnish (including polyurethane varnish), water-based, or lacquer, but be careful with lacquer because the thinner in it may blister the finish if applied really wet. In all cases, applying thinned coats produces better, more level, results. Oil is not as effective as a hard, film-building finish and could darken the wood unevenly and undesirably as the oil ages and darkens.
- Abrade the surface before applying restorer, paste wax or finish. Use sandpaper if you want to level the surface. Steel wool and Scotch-Brite pads merely round over unevenness. Abrading removes the top surface, which serves doubly to clean dirt. Don't abrade through any color, whether in the wood or in the finish, or you may lose control and end up having to refinish.
- Amalgamate the finish and respread. This can be done only with shellac and lacquer. Wipe or brush an appropriate solvent over the surface to soften or liquefy the finish, then smooth it level.

## TABLETOPS & THE NEED
## TO REFINISH

It's a widespread myth among woodworkers that the way to reduce, and
maybe even prevent, warping is to finish both sides of the wood. I don't have
any objection to finishing the underside
and inside, but doing so isn't going to
have any significant impact on warping;
the moisture content of the wood is
going to adjust to the surrounding at-
mosphere anyway. It's keeping the finish
on the exposed side in good shape that
makes the biggest difference.

Have you ever noticed that warps
in tabletops, deck boards, siding, floor-
boards and even cutting boards are
almost always concave on the top or
exposed side? And that this is the case
no matter which side of the wood
(heartwood, sapwood or quartersawn) is
up or out, or whether one or both sides
of the wood is finished?

The explanation is that the top or
exposed side was wetted and allowed
to dry repeatedly over a long period
of time and the finish (or paint) wasn't
in good enough shape to prevent the
water from getting to the wood. The
continued wetting and drying of just
one side caused compression shrinkage
(or "compression set").

Compression shrinkage is a technical term used by wood technologists to
describe a condition in which the cylindrical cells of cellulose in wood are not
allowed to expand when moisture is ab-
sorbed, so they get compressed into oval
shapes. Compression shrinkage explains
how screws work loose in wood, and why
wooden handles become loose in ham-
mers and hatchets. It also explains splits
in the ends of boards and checks in the
middle of boards in addition to warping.

When water enters wood, the cellulose cell walls swell. If the wetting
is only on one side, and the thickness
of the wood prevents the cells from
expanding, they become compressed
into oval shapes. When the wood dries,

Tabletops are often exposed to spills or wiped down with a damp cloth. If the finish is deteriorated, water can get into the wood and, over time, cause enough compression shrinkage to
warp it concave. This type of warp has nothing to do with which side of the wood (heartwood,
sapwood or quartersawn) is up or whether the finish was applied to one or both sides.

Wood floors are often kept clean by wet mopping, and if the finish isn't kept in good shape the
boards will cup due to compression shrinkage. Every floorboard throughout this second-floor
apartment has cupped, and the boards were, of course, laid randomly.

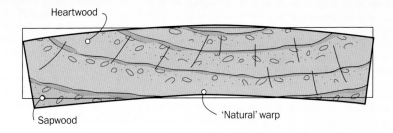

Heartwood

Sapwood

'Natural' warp

Compression shrinkage

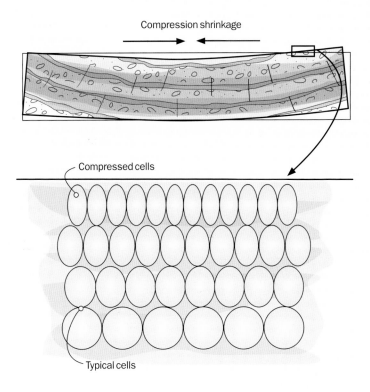

Compressed cells

Typical cells

Antique plainsawn wood can be expected to have shrunk and warped around the rings as the surrounding conditions in buildings have become drier over the last 150 years. Most antique tabletops were made with the heartwood up because it's the better side, with more good wood exposed. So it would be expected that old tabletops would bow rather than cup. But the opposite has happened in almost all cases. The fact that the underside was not finished can't possibly have anything to do with the warping.

Wood is composed of cylindrical cells of cellulose that are compressed into oval shapes when the wood is exposed repeatedly to cycles of wetting and drying out. The compression becomes permanent, and if the exposure is to one side only, the wood warps and eventually splits. Spills and exposure to damp washcloths are the primary causes of warping in tabletops.

the cells don't resume their cylindrical shapes and that side shrinks a little. Each time the one side is wetted and dries out it shrinks a little more. Repeated wetting and drying of one side eventually leads to that side cupping, and if the cycle continues long enough, the wood splits and checks.

Tabletops are commonly wiped with a damp cloth to clean spills and sticky dirt. If the finish is allowed to deteriorate to the point where it no longer prevents water penetration (or if the finish is too thin to prevent water penetration), warping and eventual splitting

result. More than any other furniture surface, the finish on tabletops needs to be kept in good condition.

Compression shrinkage has been well understood by wood technologists for decades, but none of them carried it to its logical conclusion to explain warping until Carey Howlett did so in a paper he presented to the Wooden Artifacts Group of AIC (The American Institute for Conservation of Historic and Artistic Works) in 1995. You can read the paper online at http://aic. stanford.edu/sg/wag/1995/WAG_95_ howlett.pdf.

Interestingly, understanding the cause of warps in tabletops leads to the counter-intuitive but effective method for correcting warps. Hold the board in clamps across the grain to keep the wood from expanding. Then wet the convex side, usually the bottom side of tabletops, many times, letting it dry thoroughly after each wetting. The convex side will slowly shrink, bringing the board flat.

# Caring for Furniture

Furniture care is a subject you're probably not very interested in, but it's a pretty sure bet that the people to whom you give or sell your projects find it very interesting. In fact, "How do I care for it?" is probably the first question they ask you.

If you give them an intelligent answer, their respect for you grows, but if you fumble around and show you don't really understand the subject, they may lose some confidence in you. There's no reason for this to happen because there are really only two things you need to know: the causes of damage and how to avoid them, and which furniture polish to recommend.

## CAUSES OF DAMAGE

The two elements that cause the most damage to furniture, especially to the finish, are light and physical abuse. No one can keep furniture totally away from light, but furniture can be kept away from bright light near windows which causes finishes to deteriorate faster than they would otherwise. To see what light does to finishes, compare the condition of an old finish protected from light under some hardware with the finish around it.

So the first instruction you should give is, "If you want the finish to stay in good shape for as long as possible, keep the furniture away from bright light, especially direct sunlight."

The second is, "Discipline your children and pets so they don't abuse the furniture, and use tablecloths, place mats, and coasters to protect the finish from scratches and water rings."

## FURNITURE-CARE PRODUCTS

There's more hype, myth and misinformation about furniture polishes and

The four types of furniture-care products are (from the two containers at left) simply a petroleum distillate with an added scent, (in the middle) an emulsification of petroleum distillate and water, (aerosols at right) petroleum distillate and silicone oil usually made into an emulsification with water, and paste wax.

waxes than about any other product related to furniture. Most of the problem is created by the suppliers themselves.

Here are the facts.

Furniture-care products do five things more or less well:

- Add shine to a dull surface
- Add scratch resistance
- Aid in dusting
- Aid in cleaning
- Add a pleasant scent to a room

No furniture polish or wax replaces natural oil in the wood (only a few exotic woods ever had it in the first place), feeds or moisturizes the wood, feeds or moisturizes the finish or builds up (unless, of course, the excess isn't wiped off). No furniture polish or wax does any harm to the wood or finish, either. Furniture polishes and waxes are totally inert.

In fact, furniture-care products don't really do much at all, and the United States and, to a lesser extent, Canada are the only countries where these prod-

ucts are used to any great extent. Most people in Europe and Japan just wipe their furniture with a damp cloth when it gets dusty or dirty.

So you could simply advise your family member, friend of customer, "You don't need to do anything at all except keep the furniture clean by wiping now and then with a damp cloth." But this probably won't work because people are conditioned to want to "use" something, to do something "good" for their furniture.

So, to understand the differences in the furniture-care products they could use, let's look at the ingredients in them and see what each does.

Besides the added scent, which does nothing for the furniture but rewards people for their dusting effort by making their house smell nice, furniture-care products are composed of one or more of four basic ingredients: slow evaporating petroleum-distillate solvent, water, wax and silicone oil.

Light is a prime cause of finish deterioration. Here you can see that the finish protected under the hardware is in near-perfect condition, while the finish exposed to light for about 100 years is badly crazed.

The furniture polishes that clean best are emulsifications of water and petroleum-distillate solvent. These polishes are usually packaged in aerosol spray cans and are always initially milky-white in color.

• Petroleum-distillate solvents used in furniture polishes are essentially slow-evaporating paint thinner. This liquid adds shine and scratch resistance only until it evaporates (usually within a few hours), helps pick up dust and cleans grease and wax. It has no cleaning effect on water-soluble dirt such as sticky fingerprints or soft drink spills.

Most clear polishes on the market, those commonly sold as lemon or some other nice-smelling oil and packaged in clear plastic containers, are composed of this single ingredient.

• Water evaporates too rapidly to be effective at adding shine or scratch resistance, but it helps pick up dust, and it's a great cleaner for most types of dirt. In many liquid and so-called "cream" furniture polishes, and in some liquid and paste waxes, water is added to improve cleaning ability. You can recognize these products by their milky-white color (they are emulsifications like milk is an emulsification of water and animal fat). Most are packaged in aerosol-spray containers.

• Wax is a solid substance at room temperature and is by far the most effective of the four ingredients at adding shine and scratch protection over a long period of time because it doesn't evaporate. But wax is hard to apply (because of the effort necessary to wipe off the

excess) and there's no reason to apply it very often, so it's not effective for dusting, cleaning or adding scent.

Sometimes wax is added to liquid polishes, and you can identify these by the settling that occurs over time — polishes containing wax have to be shaken before use. Clearly, these polishes will be more effective at adding long-lasting shine and scratch protection than polishes that don't contain wax, but more effort will be required to remove the excess from the surface.

• Silicone oil is a synthetic oil similar to mineral oil in the sense that it is totally inert and doesn't evaporate, but silicone oil is slipperier and bends light better than mineral oil. The first quality makes furniture polishes that contain this oil extremely effective at reducing scratches and the second makes finished wood appear richer and deeper.

Most aerosol-spray polishes contain silicone oil, though rarely is this admitted. Silicone oil has been given a bad reputation by furniture refinishers and museum conservators due to the added difficulty they have refinishing furniture treated with this oil. But consumers love silicone-oil polishes because they keep furniture looking good between polishings better than anything except wax, and they're easy to use.

Most polishes that contain silicone oil also contain petroleum distillates and water, so they're good cleaners.

## HOW TO CHOOSE

So how do you make sense of this for the recipients of your projects? Easy.

If they just want something for dusting, choose any liquid furniture polish. I recommend the simple petroleum-distillate polish.

If they want something that will clean in addition to picking up dust, choose any milky-white furniture polish — virtually all polishes in aerosol containers except Scott's Liquid Gold.

If they want maximum scratch resistance and richer depth without the work involved with using paste wax, choose a polish that contains silicone oil — virtually all polishes in aerosol-spray containers except Endust and Scott's Liquid Gold.

If they want to add shine and protect an old, deteriorated surface from abrasive damage, choose paste wax — because the other possibilities either evaporate too quickly (petroleum distillate) or highlight the cracks in the finish (silicone oil). Dusting and cleaning will have to be done separately with a damp cloth because petroleum-distillate solvents remove wax.

# Outdoor Finishes

The need to protect wood outdoors is much greater than the need to protect it indoors because of exposure to sunlight and rain. These cause wood to gray, split, warp and rot; and moist conditions make the growth of mildew possible.

You can use paint, stain, clear finish, water repellant and preservative to prevent or retard damage to exterior wood. But first, it's helpful to understand the causes of the damage.

## EXTERIOR DAMAGE

Sunlight contains strong ultraviolet light, which is very destructive over time. UV light destroys the lignin that glues the cellulose wood cells together, and rain then washes the lignin away. Because the lignin contains the extractives that give wood its distinctive coloring, the wood turns silvery gray on the surface when the lignin is gone.

Sunlight also heats the surface of the wood and draws out moisture, causing shrinkage. This leads to splitting and warping, and these are made worse by rain when it comes in contact with only one side of the wood—as on decks, tabletops and exterior doors. The water makes the surface cells swell, but the thickness of the wood prevents the surface from expanding. The cells are forced to compress to oval shapes, and they hold these shapes even when dry.

This phenomenon is called "compression shrinkage" or "compression set." Compression shrinkage causes wood to warp and split as the exposed side continues to shrink a little more each time it goes through the wetting and drying cycle.

Rain is partially responsible for rotting and the growth of mildew, because

This front door faces west with no trees or other obstructions to block afternoon sunlight. You can see that the door is in good shape at the top where the deep recess in the framing protects it. But the condition worsens progressively from there down because of contact with both sunlight and rain. The best solution is to coat the door with a marine varnish high in UV-absorber content, and sand back and recoat whenever the varnish begins to dull.

The combination of sunlight and rain causes wood to turn silvery gray. If you like the gray color, and you aren't having other problems, you can leave the wood unprotected. The grayed surface is very effective at blocking further degradation below. UV light erodes wood at only about 1/4" per century.

Quartersawn wood (right) is much more resistant to splitting than plainsawn wood (left). If you have a choice, always use quartersawn wood in exterior exposures. The two boards shown here are from a cedar tabletop left outside and unfinished for about eight years.

both require moisture to occur. Rain is also indirectly responsible for a visually similar damage — insect infestation — because insects require moisture to thrive.

The heartwood of redwood, cedar and some hardwoods is naturally resistant to rotting. Some softwoods are pressure treated with chemicals to make them resistant to rotting. These woods have the familiar dull green or dull brown coloring. Sapwood and non-pressure-treated pine and fir are not resistant to rotting.

There are five different types of coatings you can use to protect against the problems caused by sunlight and rain: paint, stain, clear finish, water repellant and preservative. You can buy any of the first four types of coatings with a preservative included to retard mildew, or you can sometimes buy a concentrated preservative separately and add it yourself.

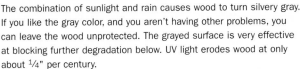

The mildew on the lower part of this board is a dark fungus that develops in moist conditions, especially in sheltered areas away from sunlight. You can prevent mildew by applying a wood preservative or a coating that contains a preservative. You can remove mildew by pressure washing or applying household bleach diluted with two to four parts water. Mildew causes little harm to the wood, but it looks bad.

Rot is very destructive to wood as is obvious in this photo. Pressure-treated wood and the heartwood of redwood, cedar and a number of exotic woods including teak and ipe resist rot. A wood preservative that is not pressure-injected is fairly ineffective at preventing rot on non-rot-resistant woods.

## PAINT

Paint is the most effective coating for protecting wood. The thick film blocks water penetration and the pigment blocks UV light. You can find wood siding that is in perfect shape after 200 years because it has been protected continuously with well-maintained coats of paint.

There are two large categories of paint: oil-based and water-based (latex). Because oil-based paint wears better than latex paint, it is best for objects that see a lot of abuse such as chairs and picnic tables.

Oil-based primers are also best when you are painting wood that has been exposed to the weather for a month or longer, especially if the wood has grayed. Oil-based primers penetrate deeper than latex primers, so they are better able to penetrate the degraded wood caused by the destruction of the surface lignin and bond to good wood underneath. If the wood is freshly milled or sanded, acrylic-latex primers perform well.

Latex paint is best for wood siding, because it is better than oil paint at allowing moisture vapor created inside a building to pass through. If the moisture vapor can't get through the paint layer, it builds up behind the paint and causes it to peel. (A primer coat of oil-based paint applied under latex paint is not thick enough to stop moisture penetration.)

Paint is great for siding and house trim because they can be caulked to keep water from getting into the wood and causing the paint to peel. Paint is also great for furniture and exterior doors if they don't get a lot of exposure to moisture.

But paint is a poor choice for decks and often for fences because it's rarely possible to seal off all the end grain effectively. The paint peels and requires too much work to effectively keep up.

## PIGMENTED STAIN

Pigmented stain is the next most effective coating for exterior wood. Just as with paint, it resists both moisture and UV-light damage because it contains both binder and pigment. But because there is much less of each and little or no film build, pigmented stains are not as resistant as paint.

On the other hand, the lack of film build makes maintenance easier. Usually, all that is required is a fresh application of the stain every year or two, depending on the climate and amount of exposure. There's seldom a reason to scrape, strip or sand.

There are three types of binder and two concentrations of pigment to choose from. The binders are oil-based, water-based and alkyd-based. The pigment concentrations are semi-transparent and solid color.

Oil-based stains are the most popular and easiest to use. You can brush, spray or roll on a coat and enough of it will either soak into the wood or evaporate so that you end up with very little or no film build. With no film build, there is nothing to peel, so recoating is easy. Simply clean the wood of dirt and mildew and apply another coat.

Water-based acrylic stains are popular because of their lack of odor, ability to be cleaned up easily and reduced amount of polluting solvents. But water-based stains leave a build that somewhat obscures the wood and may peel if water gets underneath. Water-based stains also show traffic patterns more easily than oil-based stains because of the thin build wearing through.

Alkyd-based stains make use of a soft varnish to attach the pigment to the wood. These stains are meant to build on the wood, but they resist peeling because they attach so well to the wood, and they are so flexible. Often, manufacturers recommend as many as three coats and instruct you to clean the surface and apply an additional coat every year or two.

The disadvantages of these stains are that they will peel anyway if the wood isn't nearly perfectly clean during initial application or recoating, and visible wear is common in high traffic areas. It's very difficult to blend these areas back in.

The primary difference between semi-transparent and solid-color stains is the amount of pigment included. Solid-color stains contain more pigment (and also more binder), so they are better at blocking UV light. But the higher pigment concentration causes greater obscuring of the wood.

Stain is usually the best choice for decks and fences, and a good choice for cedar-shingle siding and cedar shingles and shakes. Stain can also be used on furniture and doors. Alkyd, solid-color, and water-based stains tend to build on the wood, which makes them vulnerable to lap marks and peeling. Semi-transparent stain is less resistant to UV light and water, but there is no peeling so recoating is easier.

### CLEAR FINISH

Clear film-building finishes, including water-based and all types of varnish, resist water penetration well, but not UV light. Destructive UV light penetrates the film and causes the wood to degrade. The lignin that glues the cellulose cells together loses its strength, and the surface fibers separate from the rest of the wood. When this happens, the finish, which is bonded to these surface fibers, peels.

The trick to getting a clear finish to survive in UV light is to add UV absorbers, and many manufacturers supply finishes with these added. There is, however, a great deal of difference in effectiveness of various products. "Marine" finishes sold at home centers and paint stores contain much less UV absorber than marine varnishes sold at marinas.

Clear finishes sold for exterior use can be divided into three categories: marine varnish, spar varnish and oil. Water-based exterior finishes are also available, but they have not found much acceptance thus far. Marine varnish is a soft, flexible varnish with UV absorbers added. Spar varnish is a soft, flexible varnish without UV absorbers added.

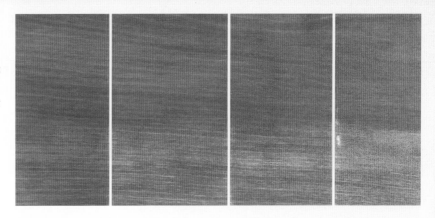

Many exterior finishes claim UV resistance, but there is a big difference in effectiveness. I applied a red dye to this panel, followed by five coats of a marine varnish bought at a marina (left), five coats of two common marine varnishes bought at a home center (center) and five coats of an interior varnish (right). Then I exposed the panel to sunlight for six months with the top half protected by newspaper. The fading of the dye shows that the home-center marine varnishes provided little more resistance to UV light than the interior varnish with no UV absorber.

Oil may or may not have UV absorbers added, but it is too thin on the surface to provide much resistance to sunlight even with them.

Linseed oil, whether raw or boiled, is also susceptible to mildew growth. In fact, mildew feeds on the fatty acids in linseed oil, so mildew develops faster than if no linseed oil had been applied. Only in very dry climates should linseed oil be considered as a finish for exterior wood.

Marine varnishes from marinas are the best clear finishes to use outdoors. They are always very glossy (for better light reflection), relatively soft (for better flexibility), and require eight or nine coats to reach maximum UV resistance. In addition, because the UV absorbers in these finishes don't prevent the finish itself from deteriorating, you will need to sand off surface deterioration (dullness, chalking and crazing) and apply a couple additional coats whenever the surface begins to deteriorate. This might be as often as once or twice a year if the finish is exposed to bright sunlight in Southern exposures.

Use marine varnish on objects where you want maximum UV resistance with a clear finish and are willing to deal with

peeling if water gets underneath the film. Use spar varnish if UV resistance isn't critical. Use oil only if you are willing to reapply it often and don't expect much UV or water resistance.

### WATER REPELLANT

Water repellants are usually mineral spirits with low-surface-tension wax or silicone added to repel water. Sometimes, they are simply thinned water-based finish.

Water repellants are fairly effective at reducing water penetration for a short time. If UV absorbers are included, water repellants block UV light for a short time. Both types of resistance wear away within months, so unless you are willing to devote a lot of attention to upkeep, the wood will gray and split almost as fast as if no coating were applied.

Water repellents provide the least protection of any exterior wood coating, but they are easy to apply because they don't leave lap marks and they don't peel.

Use water repellant on decks if you don't mind the wood graying or splitting. Use water repellant with a preservative included to fight mildew if you live in a humid climate.

# Easy Finish Repairs

All wood finishes except oil and wax are plastic materials. So you can think of a finish as a thin sheet of plastic enveloping your furniture or woodwork.

This plastic can become damaged in many ways. Sometimes the damage is so great that the finish has to be stripped and the object refinished. But other times you can repair the damage.

Following are common types of damage that you can repair fairly easily without having to call a professional touch-up specialist.

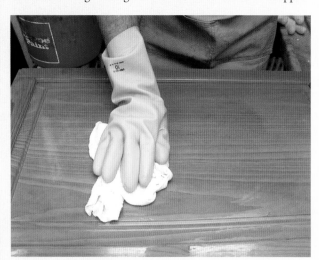

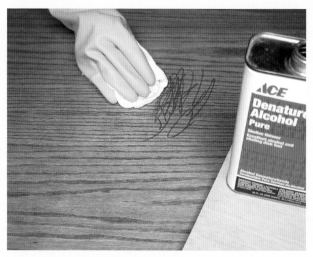

## CLEAN A DIRTY SURFACE

To clean a dirty finish, you do what you would do to clean any dirty surface: wash it. In the order of their strength here are the three most commonly available cleaning substances you can try: water, dishwater detergent and water, household ammonia and water. Whichever you use, dry the surface with a dry cloth or paper towel quickly after washing to prevent additional damage.

Water isn't nearly as effective as soap and water, which is what you should probably try first.

Household ammonia and water is a very effective cleaner. But be aware that it will dull some finishes, especially lacquer and shellac. So if you don't want to dull the finish, start with a very weak solution, say about a quarter of a cup of ammonia to a gallon of warm water. Then add more ammonia if necessary.

Here I'm washing a kitchen cabinet door with household ammonia and water to prepare the thirty-year-old finish for a "refresher" coat.

## REMOVE FELT-TIP PEN MARKS

Marks from felt-tip pens (magic markers) are usually easy to remove with denatured alcohol. Simply dampen a cloth with the alcohol and wipe away the marks. There are two cautions, however.

Denatured alcohol will dissolve shellac, so don't use the alcohol if the finish is shellac. Shellac has been used rarely since the 1920s, and when it has, it's been by amateurs or small-shop professionals. If you aren't sure, try wiping an inconspicuous area to see if you dull the finish.

Not all felt-tip-pen marks will come off with denatured alcohol, but most will. If the marks don't lift off immediately, you have a much bigger problem and making the cloth wetter won't solve it. You can try sanding out the marks, but they could go very deep. You may have to refinish or paint.

## SHINE UP A DULL FINISH

As finishes age they dull. The dulling happens more quickly if the finish is exposed to sunlight. There are several things you can do to put shine back into the surface.

The two easiest and least risky are to apply paste wax or a silicone furniture polish. Most aerosol furniture polishes contain silicone oil.

Applying paste wax can be a lot of work, but an application is fairly permanent as long as you don't then dust with furniture polish. Furniture polish contains a lot of petroleum distillate, which will remove the wax. Use a damp cloth instead for dusting.

Silicone furniture polishes are very popular with consumers because they are easy to use and add shine and scratch resistance for a week or two (until the next dusting). These polishes aren't as permanent as paste wax.

Other possibilities for adding shine are the widely available Howard's Restore-a-Finish (which is available in colors to color in nicks and scratches), oil/varnish blend and wiping varnish. Each of these is wipe-on, wipe-off, so there is little

risk of causing a problem. Still, you should try the one you choose on an inconspicuous area first.

Be sure to clean the surface before applying oil/varnish blend or wiping varnish.

Here I'm applying paste wax to a dull tabletop.

## REMOVE CRAYON MARKS

Crayons are wax, so marks are easy to remove with mineral spirits. Even a clear furniture polish may work, though it won't be as effective.

Just dampen a cloth with mineral spirits and wipe off the waxy marks as I'm doing here. Mineral spirits won't damage any finish, but it will remove wax if you have waxed the surface.

## REMOVE CANDLE WAX DRIPS

The easy way to remove drips of candle wax is to freeze the dried puddle, then pick off the lump of wax with your fingernail, as I'm doing here. Holding an ice cube in contact with the wax for 20 or 30 seconds is usually enough. If some residue wax remains on the surface, wipe it off with mineral spirits.

The not-so-easy and riskier method of removing drips of candle wax is to slowly scrape off the puddle of wax using a credit card. As you get close to the finish, lighten up on the pressure so you don't scratch it. Just before scraping the finish, switch to mineral spirits to remove the remaining wax.

## REMOVE STICKERS AND TAPE

Old stickers and tape stuck to a finish or paint can be difficult to remove. Acetone and lacquer thinner will usually work, but these will damage most finishes. So these solvents are risky to use.

Better methods are to try heat from a blow dryer or a mild solvent such as mineral spirits or naphtha. Another possibility for paper stickers is wetting them enough with water so you can rub them off using your finger. If the adhesive resists, heat it a little. Situations vary. You just have to try to see what works.

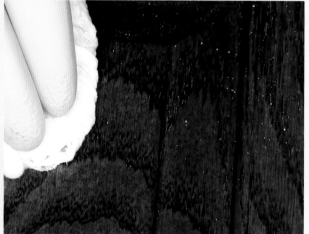

## REMOVE LATEX PAINT SPATTER

Rolling latex paint onto a wall or ceiling throws off tiny spatter that you probably won't notice until you see the little dots of paint on the furniture or cabinets you didn't cover well.

Fortunately, latex paint softens with xylene (xylol) and toluene (toluol) enough so it can be rubbed off. The commercial products Oops! and Goof Off are xylene, so you can use one of these instead.

But be aware that these solvents will usually damage water-based finish (the same chemistry as latex paint). So if you aren't sure of the finish, try the solvent on an inconspicuous area to be sure the finish doesn't dull. Water-based finishes were rarely used before the 1990s.

## COLORING A SCUFFED EDGE

It's common for the finish and color on 90° edges to be rubbed off. This problem is easy to repair using one of the widely-available colored touch-up markers. These markers are similar to magic markers, just in wood tones.

To do the repair, simply drag the marker along the damaged edge. You can go back over again if you want to make the color darker, but let the first pass dry first. Even so, you may have difficulty getting the color a lot darker because the solvent in the marker is taking off the already applied color about as fast as the marker is applying more color.

It's best to seal this color in so it isn't rubbed off easily. Do this with a quick wipe using an oil/varnish blend or wiping varnish, just on the edge so as not to leave noticeable marks on the adjoining surfaces.

You could also recoat the entire surface with one of these finishes, as described for shining up a dull finish.

## REMOVE MILDEW

Mildew forms in damp areas, and it looks like this when it gets bad. It's easy enough to wipe off the mildew, but to keep it from coming back you have to kill the spors. Do this by wiping with a cloth dampened with half-and-half household bleach and water. Then move the object to a drier area or make that room drier.

## REMOVE WHITE WATER RINGS

White marks on tabletops caused by sweaty glasses or sitting water can usually be removed, though not without some risk of damaging the finish. Professionals have access to a product called "blush remover" that restores the color to lacquer finishes. The product is sold in convenient aerosols.

The reason these aerosols aren't available for amateurs is that they can blister finishes if not used properly. If you should locate a source for a blush remover, be sure to spray just a fine mist over the water ring. Don't make the surface wet, and for sure, don't touch the surface until it dries, which can take a while.

Other than blush remover you can try coating the mark overnight with an oily substance such as mayonnaise or cooking oil. Or you can wipe over the mark with a cloth lightly dampened with denatured alcohol. Don't make the surface wet, only damp enough so you see a vapor trail of evaporating alcohol following the cloth.

These methods may work if the damage is superficial.

The method that almost always works is to abrade off the watermark. The whiteness is almost always right at the surface of the finish, so it doesn't take much. The trick is to avoid changing the sheen (gloss or satin) of the finish more than necessary. So your choice of abrasive is important.

## REMOVE LIGHT CRAZING

The only way to remove light crazing (roughness in the finish) is to sand the finish level using very fine sandpaper. Then apply paste wax or some sort of finish to put the shine back in. Any finish is alright to use, but a wipe-on, wipe-off finish such as wiping varnish or oil/varnish blend will cause the fewest problems.

Every situation is different. Here are some suggestions for abrasives you can use: toothpaste and your finger; #0000 steel wool and some mineral oil or paste wax to reduce the scratching; a white, gray or other very fine nylon abrasive pad with an oil or wax lubricant.

Be aware that heat marks also show up white but are usually more difficult to remove (though the methods are the same). The damage may go deeper into the finish.

Black rings are in the wood and can't be removed without removing the finish first.

## DISGUISE SCRATCHES

Scratches are of three types: a clear finish restores the color; a clear finish darkens the scratch making it show worse; or the color has to be "painted in."

You can easily test to see which type of scratch you are dealing with by dabbing a liquid onto the scratch. Mineral spirits (paint thinner) would be best because it would simultaneously remove any wax or residue furniture polish. But mineral spirits isn't always handy. Liquid from your mouth is available, though, and it's what I almost always use.

If the liquid puts the color back, you can apply any finish to make the scratch disappear, or at least bring the color back. Wiping varnish or oil/varnish blend will cause the fewest problems. Wipe the finish over the entire surface, and wipe off the excess.

If the scratch darkens, you should use paste wax. It won't darken the scratch as much as a liquid will.

If nothing happens when you wet the scratch, the only way to repair it is to paint it using a fine artist's brush and some colorant. Any colorant will work as long as it has a binder to glue the pigment to the wood, but it usually takes experience to get the colors right.

Doing this type of finish repair (and also the next one involving filling gouges) is the most skilled area of finishing. If the object with the problem is important to you, it might be best to hire a professional touch-up specialist.

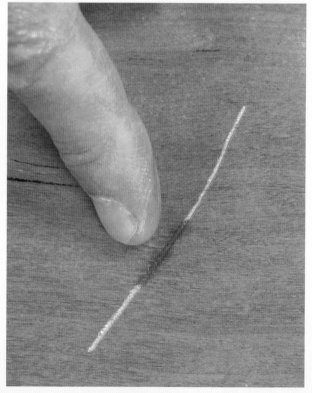

## FILL GOUGES

There are several methods professionals use to fill gouges. The easiest is with two-part epoxy in solid (not liquid) form. The most convenient packaging is in sticks that resemble large tootsie rolls, with one part in the center and the other on the outside.

Sometimes you can find solid two-part epoxy sticks in colors, in which case you should choose a color that most closely matches the lightest color in the wood you are filling. If you are limited to a neutral-color epoxy, you will have to color it after it has hardened in the gouge or add color to it as you knead it.

The steps as illustrated are straightforward. But, as with repairing scratches, experience is critical for achieving good results. So you should consider hiring a specialist if the surface is critical.

1     Cut epoxy fill

2     Knead together

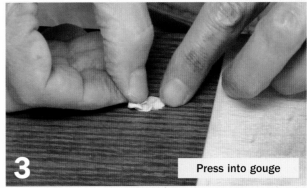
3     Press into gouge

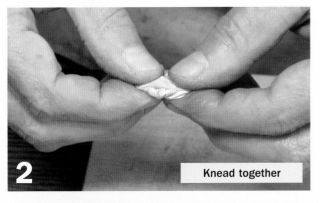
4     Flatten

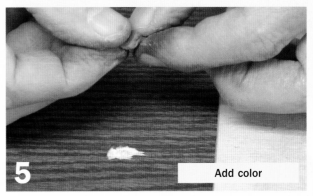
5     Add color

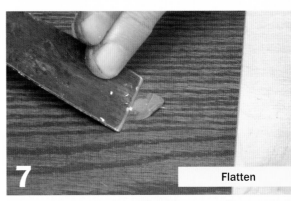
6     Press into gouge

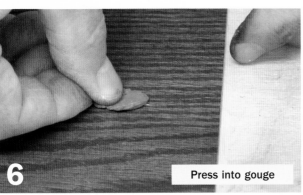
7     Flatten

# Cleaning and Storing Brushes

**1** To clean a brush used in oil or oil-based varnish, first rinse it in mineral spirits (paint thinner) by scrunching the bristles against the bottom the container. Then shake out the excess thinner and rinse again in clean mineral spirits.

**2** Following at least two rinsings in mineral spirits (the second in clean mineral spirits), rinse in lacquer thinner or acetone to remove the oily mineral spirits. You could do all the rinsings in lacquer thinner or acetone, but they are more expensive.

**3** Finish the cleaning by washing with soap and water until the soap lathers easily. The lacquer-thinner or acetone rinsing makes this happen much quicker. For brushes used in water-based finish, this soap-and-water washing is the only step you need for cleaning. Don't rinse this brush in mineral spirits or lacquer thinner.

**4** Finally, wrap the brush in the holder it came in or in absorbent paper and secure the wrap with a rubber band or masking tape. You can then hang the brush or store it in a drawer. The bristles will dry straight and remain clean.

There are four categories of brushes. From left to right: foam brush, inexpensive "chip" brush, synthetic-bristle brush and natural bristle brush. Foam and chip brushes are usually thrown away after a project because it can be more expensive to clean them than to buy a new one. Foam brushes can be difficult to use on three-dimensional objects, but foam brushes don't shed bristles. Chip brushes shed bristles and become limp in water-based products. Synthetic-bristle brushes can be used with any finish, but are uniquely suited to water-based products. Natural-bristle brushes are for solvent-based products. Their bristles lose their spring in water-based products.

## TIP

To pour from a full solvent can without splashing the solvent all over, pour with the spout at the top.

# Understanding Wood

## INTRODUCTION

Species of wood differ significantly in figure, grain and color. These differences affect the way stains and finishes look on them. Because wood is the canvas you're working on when you apply a finish, it's wise to have some understanding of the differences so you can choose a wood that will give you the end result you want. Too often people choose a wood for cost or because it's readily available only to realize after building the project that achieving the desired look with that wood is very difficult or even impossible.

## FIVE CATEGORIES OF WOOD

There are countless wood species. The easiest way to make sense of them is to group them into five large categories:

- Softwoods — for example, pine, fir and cedar.
- Coarse-grain hardwoods — for example, oak, ash and elm.
- Medium-grain hardwoods — for example, walnut, mahogany and butternut.
- Fine-grain hardwoods — for example, maple, cherry and poplar.
- Exotic woods, which are those, other than mahogany, that grow in jungle environments.

## SOFTWOOD CHARACTERISTICS

- Visually pronounced alternating spring- and summer-growth rings. The spring growth is soft and usually appears lighter than the harder summer growth. The spring growth absorbs more stain and finish than does the summer growth. It often takes more coats of finish to get an even sheen across both growths than with hardwoods, and the spring

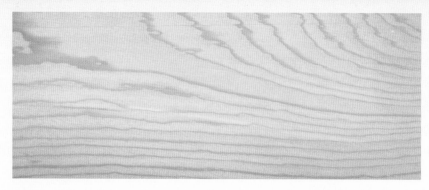

PINE

FIR

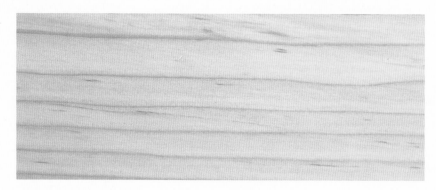

AROMATIC CEDAR

growth often gets darker than the summer growth when stain is applied. The lighter/darker areas reverse.

- Random areas that stain darker. The uneven coloring when a stain is applied is called "blotching." The best

method for avoiding blotching in softwoods is to use a gel stain.

- No visual pores. The surface with a finish applied is therefore perfectly flat; there isn't any pitting.

## COARSE-GRAIN HARDWOOD CHARACTERISTICS

- Visually pronounced alternating spring- and summer-growth rings. The spring growth is pitted with large "pores," and it hollows easier with sandpaper than the summer growth, which is smooth and hard. You should therefore not sand with just your fingers backing your sandpaper or you'll hollow out these areas. Unless you fill the pitting level with the summer growth, finishes follow the contours revealing the coarseness of the wood. This isn't bad; in fact, it is a desirable quality of the wood. Coarse-grain hardwoods are rarely filled.

- The coarse spring growth stains darker than the smooth summer growth. When you wipe off excess stain from coarse-grain woods, more stain remains lodged in the pitting of the spring growth causing it to be darker. The only way to get an even coloring on these woods is to spray the stain and not wipe it.

- The angle that boards are cut from tree trunks makes a big visual difference. When boards are cut tangentially from tree trunks, called "plainsawn," the alternating spring- and summer-growth areas are wide. When boards are cut radially from tree trunks called "quartersawn" (because the trunk is quartered and then sawn into boards), the alternating spring- and summer-growth areas are narrow. In the case of oak, radial cuts reveal "medulary rays" a unique visual effect often referred to colloquially as "tiger stripes." These areas are very dense and are difficult to color.

OAK

ASH

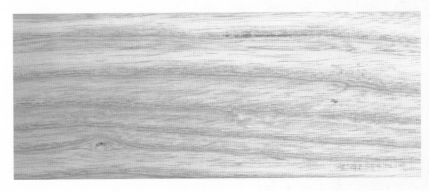

ELM

QUARTER-SAWN OAK

## MEDIUM-GRAIN HARDWOOD CHARACTERISTICS

- Much reduced visual difference between spring growth and summer growth, compared to softwoods and coarse-grain hardwoods. The pitting of the pores is less pronounced than in coarse-grain woods and usually more evenly spaced. Therefore, it's not so easy to hollow out areas if you back sandpaper with just your fingers, though you should still use a flat block when sanding by hand.

- The coloring is more even than with softwoods or coarse-grain hardwoods when a stain is applied. The pores become a little darker (and thus highlighted, creating the illusion of more depth), but not nearly so much as with coarse-grain woods.

- The difference in appearance between plainsawn and quartersawn is not as pronounced as with coarse-grain woods, so boards are rarely quartersawn on purpose.

- Most elegant when the pores are filled. These are the woods that are most often filled because they take on an elegant appearance when reflected light isn't broken up by the pores.

WALNUT

MAHOGANY

BUTTERNUT

## FINE-GRAIN HARDWOOD CHARACTERISTICS

- Much reduced visual difference between spring growth and summer growth. The pores are very small and barely visible and are usually filled level with just the finish. No extra step is required to accomplish this. You should still use a sanding block when sanding large flat surfaces by hand even though there aren't any softer areas to be hollowed out.
- The overall denseness of these woods makes them difficult to stain dark except with dye stains.
- There's not enough difference between plainsawn and quartersawn to make it worthwhile to quartersaw these woods.
- Most fine-grain hardwoods blotch when stain is applied. Some, such as cherry, also blotch mildly with just a finish, no stain.
- More than other woods, maple can display a very interesting and desirable figure, the two most common being bird's eye maple and curly maple.

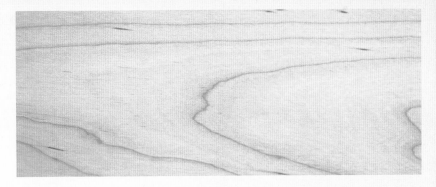

MAPLE

CHERRY

POPLAR

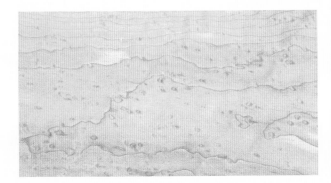

BIRD'S-EYE MAPLE

CURLY MAPLE

These are examples of the first four categories of wood species. From left to right: pine, oak, mahogany, maple. The bottom half of each is stained with the same stain. It's quite obvious when the woods are put next to each other that woods in different categories can't be make to look alike with just a stain. They differ too much in figure, grain and color. You will have much greater success getting woods within a category to look similar.

## EXOTIC HARDWOOD CHARACTERISTICS

- Most exotic woods, those that grow in jungle environments, are darker in color. They are also usually very dense, heavy and relatively expensive, and many are available only in smaller pieces, not large boards. The larger market for these woods is for woodturnings and for use as inlay. Many exotic woods are sliced into thin veneer sheets for use as inlay.

- An important characteristic of most exotic woods is their natural oiliness. You can feel the oiliness on the surface. This oily resin will interfere with the drying of oils and varnishes, so it's usually wise to wipe off the surface oil with naphtha just before applying the first coat of one of these finishes. Apply the finish quickly after the solvent evaporates, before the interior oil has time to rise back to the surface.

TEAK

EAST INDIAN ROSEWOOD

GABON EBONY

## HEARTWOOD AND SAPWOOD

A characteristic of most hardwoods, especially the darker ones, is a clear distinction between heartwood and sapwood. Sapwood is nearly white and is from the outer circumference of the tree trunk. Heartwood is from the center of the tree trunk. When boards are cut from logs, there may be sapwood on one edge or on both edges. You can cut off the sapwood, or you can use it to decorative advantage.

Sapwood can be stained to look like heartwood, but most of the coloring steps to achieve this are done between coats of finish. This is advanced finishing. Please refer to one of my other books.

## SOLID WOOD AND VENEER

Boards cut from a tree are called "solid" wood. When the tree trunk is sliced into thin sheets, these are called "veneer."

You can usually tell that a board is solid wood by looking at the end grain and lining the spring and summer growth rings up with the grain on the flat surface. With the exception of buying veneer in sheets to glue yourself, veneer is usually sold glued to plywood or MDF (medium density fiberboard). You can usually identify veneered plywood or MDF by looking at the edge.

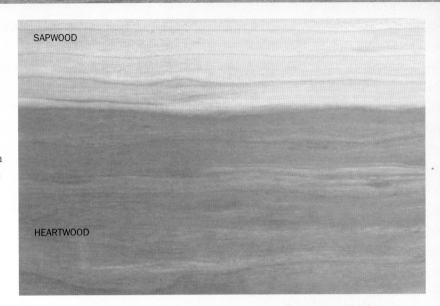

SAPWOOD

HEARTWOOD

SOLID

VENEER ON PLYWOOD

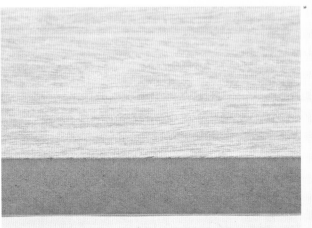

VENEER ON MDF

## MACHINE MARKS

It's important to understand that when wood is "milled," whether at the lumber mill, lumber yard or machined in your shop, marks are left that have to be sanded out. These are called "mill marks" or "machine marks."

The marks, which may be in the form of scratches but are most often compressed areas, can be difficult to see. It's helpful to wet the surface to make them stand out. Water raises the grain of the wood. So if you don't want to do this, use mineral spirits or alcohol. If you are going to sand heavily anyway, the only objection to water is that it takes longer to dry.

## PANELS SHRINK REVEALING UNSTAINED AND UNFINISHED LINES

Wood shrinks and expands across the grain, not along the grain. So panels inserted in frames can shrink enough, especially in winter when it's dry, to reveal uncolored stripes at the edges. This panel is painted on both sides. Neither clear finish nor paint stops the shrinking. The wood always adjusts to the ambient humidity.

# INDEX

# IDEAS. INSTRUCTION. INSPIRATION.

These and other great **Popular Woodworking** products are available at your local bookstore, woodworking store or online supplier.

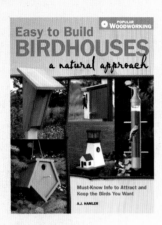

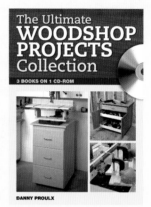

## EASY TO BUILD BIRDHOUSES
BY A.J. HAMLER

Projects range from traditional designs to a lighthouse, a cottage and a football helmet and more! Fun to build and fun to watch the birds move into their new home!

paperback · 144 pages

## ARTS & CRAFTS FURNITURE ANYONE CAN MAKE
BY DAVID THIEL

By reducing classic Arts & Crafts furniture designs to their basics, then adding simple, screw-together joinery, anyone can build great-looking furniture. Create a piece of furniture in a weekend that you'll proudly display for years.

paperback · 160 pages

## POPULAR WOODWORKING MAGAZINE

Whether learning a new hobby or perfecting your craft, *Popular Woodworking Magazine* has expert information to teach the skill, not just the project. Find the latest issue on newsstands, or order online at www.popularwoodworking.com.

## THE ULTIMATE WOODSHOP PROJECT COLLECTION
CD-ROM, BOOKS BY DANNY PROULX

This CD-ROM gives you all the information you need to make your shop the best it can be.

This disc includes the full book  content from: *Building Woodshop Workstations, Toolboxes & Wookbenches* and *50 Jigs & Fixtures.*
CD-ROM

---

Visit **www.popularwoodworking.com** to see more woodworking information by the experts.

| Recent Articles | Featured Product | Note from the Editor |
|---|---|---|
| Read the five most recent articles from Popular Woodworking Books. | **Made By Hand** $21.95 | **Welcome to Books & More** |

**Recent Articles**

Read the five most recent articles from Popular Woodworking Books.

- **Kitchen Makeovers - Pull-Out Pantry Design & Construction**
- **Woodshop Lust Tom Rosati's Woodshop**
- **Woodshop Lust David Thiel's Woodshop**
- **Wood Finishing Simplified Strictly, Stickley Oak**
- **Wood Finishing Simplified In a Pickle** (Whitewash on Oak or Pine)

**Featured Product**

**Made By Hand**
$21.95

*Made By Hand* takes you right to the bench and shows you how to start building furniture using hand tools. By working through the six projects in this book, you'll learn the basics of hand-tool woodworking and how to use the tools effectively and efficiently, then add joinery skills and design complexity. The accompanying DVD includes valuable insight into the tools themselves and a look at the techniques that make these tools work so well.

**Note from the Editor**

**Welcome to Books & More**
We've got the latest reviews and free sample excerpts from our favorite woodworking books, plus news on the newest releases. Check out the savings at our Woodworker's Book Shop, and don't miss out on building your Wish List for the holidays. If you missed our newsletter's **"Print Is Dead"** poll results, check them here, and subscribe (below) to our newsletter to receive special sale items and book reviews not found anywhere else.

– David Baker-Thiel, Executive Editor
*Popular Woodworking Books*

A woodworking education can come in many forms, including books, magazines, videos and community feedback. At Popular Woodworking we've got them all. Visit our website at www.popularwoodworking.com to follow our blogs, read about the newest tools and books and join our community. We want to know what you're building.

Sign up to receive our weekly newsletter at http://popularwoodworking.com/newsletters/